D0821642

Libya

Other Books of Related Interest:

Opposing Viewpoints Series

Canada

China

Iran

Israel

At Issue Series

What Is Humanity's Greatest Challenge?

Is Iran a Threat to Global Security?

Current Controversies Series

Oil

The World Economy

"Congress shall make
no law . . . abridging
the freedom of speech,
or of the press."

First Amendment to the US Constitution

The basic foundation of our democracy is the First Amendment guarantee of freedom of expression. The Opposing Viewpoints series is dedicated to the concept of this basic freedom and the idea that it is more important to practice it than to enshrine it.

Libya

Noah Berlatsky, Book Editor

GREENHAVEN PRESS
A part of Gale, Cengage Learning

Detroit • New York • San Francisco • New Haven, Conn • Waterville, Maine • London

Elizabeth Des Chenes, *Managing Editor*

© 2012 Greenhaven Press, a part of Gale, Cengage Learning.

Gale and Greenhaven Press are registered trademarks used herein under license.

For more information, contact:
Greenhaven Press
27500 Drake Rd.
Farmington Hills, MI 48331-3535
Or you can visit our Internet site at gale.cengage.com

For product information and technology assistance, contact us at

Gale Customer Support, 1-800-877-4253
For permission to use material from this text or product, submit all requests online at www.cengage.com/permissions

Further permissions questions can be emailed to permissionrequest@cengage.com

Articles in Greenhaven Press anthologies are often edited for length to meet page requirements. In addition, original titles of these works are changed to clearly present the main thesis and to explicitly indicate the author's opinion. Every effort is made to ensure that Greenhaven Press accurately reflects the original intent of the authors. Every effort has been made to trace the owners of copyrighted material.

Cover Image © Pascal Rateau/Shutterstock.com.

LIBRARY OF CONGRESS CATALOGING-IN-PUBLICATION DATA

Libya / Noah Berlatsky, book editor.
    p. cm. -- (Opposing viewpoints)
    Includes bibliographical references and index.
    ISBN 978-0-7377-6031-6 (hardcover) -- ISBN 978-0-7377-6032-3 (pbk.)
    1. Libya--Politics and government--1969- 2. Libya--Foreign relations--United States. 3. United States--Foreign relations--Libya. 4. Human rights--Libya. I. Berlatsky, Noah. II. Series: Opposing viewpoints series (Unnumbered)
    DT236.L532 2012
    961.204'2--dc23
                                                                    2011034693

Printed in the United States of America
1 2 3 4 5 6 7 16 15 14 13 12

Contents

Chapter 3: What Issues Impact Libya's Resistance Movement?

Chapter 4: What Should the US Role in Libya Be?

Why Consider
Opposing Viewpoints?

> *"The only way in which a human being can make some approach to knowing the whole of a subject is by hearing what can be said about it by persons of every variety of opinion and studying all modes in which it can be looked at by every character of mind. No wise man ever acquired his wisdom in any mode but this."*
>
> John Stuart Mill

In our media-intensive culture it is not difficult to find differing opinions. Thousands of newspapers and magazines and dozens of radio and television talk shows resound with differing points of view. The difficulty lies in deciding which opinion to agree with and which "experts" seem the most credible. The more inundated we become with differing opinions and claims, the more essential it is to hone critical reading and thinking skills to evaluate these ideas. Opposing Viewpoints books address this problem directly by presenting stimulating debates that can be used to enhance and teach these skills. The varied opinions contained in each book examine many different aspects of a single issue. While examining these conveniently edited opposing views, readers can develop critical thinking skills such as the ability to compare and contrast authors' credibility, facts, argumentation styles, use of persuasive techniques, and other stylistic tools. In short, the Opposing Viewpoints Series is an ideal way to attain the higher-level thinking and reading skills so essential in a culture of diverse and contradictory opinions.

In addition to providing a tool for critical thinking, Opposing Viewpoints books challenge readers to question their own strongly held opinions and assumptions. Most people form their opinions on the basis of upbringing, peer pressure, and personal, cultural, or professional bias. By reading carefully balanced opposing views, readers must directly confront new ideas as well as the opinions of those with whom they disagree. This is not to argue simplistically that everyone who reads opposing views will—or should—change his or her opinion. Instead, the series enhances readers' understanding of their own views by encouraging confrontation with opposing ideas. Careful examination of others' views can lead to the readers' understanding of the logical inconsistencies in their own opinions, perspective on why they hold an opinion, and the consideration of the possibility that their opinion requires further evaluation.

Evaluating Other Opinions

To ensure that this type of examination occurs, Opposing Viewpoints books present all types of opinions. Prominent spokespeople on different sides of each issue as well as well-known professionals from many disciplines challenge the reader. An additional goal of the series is to provide a forum for other, less known, or even unpopular viewpoints. The opinion of an ordinary person who has had to make the decision to cut off life support from a terminally ill relative, for example, may be just as valuable and provide just as much insight as a medical ethicist's professional opinion. The editors have two additional purposes in including these less known views. One, the editors encourage readers to respect others' opinions—even when not enhanced by professional credibility. It is only by reading or listening to and objectively evaluating others' ideas that one can determine whether they are worthy of consideration. Two, the inclusion of such viewpoints encourages the important critical thinking skill of objectively evaluating an author's credentials and bias. This evaluation will illuminate an author's reasons for taking a particular stance on an issue and will aid in readers' evaluation of the author's ideas.

It is our hope that these books will give readers a deeper understanding of the issues debated and an appreciation of the complexity of even seemingly simple issues when good and honest people disagree. This awareness is particularly important in a democratic society such as ours in which people enter into public debate to determine the common good. Those with whom one disagrees should not be regarded as enemies but rather as people whose views deserve careful examination and may shed light on one's own.

Thomas Jefferson once said that "difference of opinion leads to inquiry, and inquiry to truth." Jefferson, a broadly educated man, argued that "if a nation expects to be ignorant and free . . . it expects what never was and never will be." As individuals and as a nation, it is imperative that we consider the opinions of others and examine them with skill and discernment. The Opposing Viewpoints series is intended to help readers achieve this goal.

David L. Bender and Bruno Leone,
Founders

Introduction

"While actually doing some good for his people and his country, Qaddafi has been ruthless towards his opposition and has courted the hatred of the West."

—Bonnie Cordes,
Qaddafi: Idealist and
Revolutionary Philanthropist, 1986

Muammar Gaddafi, the former leader of Libya, was one of the world's most divisive leaders. "Few world leaders in modern times have stirred as much controversy as the charismatic Gaddafi. In the early years of the 1 September Revolution, he was celebrated as a hero by the revolutionaries and liberation movements of the world. At the same time, he was roundly condemned as a meddling, destabilizing, and dangerous influence, if not a terrorist, by many governments in and out of the region," according to the *Biographical Encyclopedia of the Modern Middle East and North Africa.*

Gaddafi was born in 1942 into a Bedouin tribe engaged in animal herding. As a young man, he was inspired by the nationalist ideas of Egyptian leader Gamal Abdel Nasser. By the age of sixteen, he had begun to organize student demonstrations against the Libyan monarchy. To further his revolutionary goals, he entered a military academy along with other revolutionaries. He and his cohorts recruited others in the military and, on September 1, 1969, "The young officers easily seized power and proclaimed the Libyan Arab Republic," according to an entry about Gaddafi in the *Encyclopedia of World Biography.*

Gaddafi was chairman of the Revolutionary Command Council, which in practice made him the leader of the country. Gaddafi quickly moved to weaken Western influence in

Libya. He "expelled the Italian community (a colonial remnant), and forced the British, French, and Americans to withdraw from the military bases they had established on Libyan soil," according to the entry on Gaddafi in the *Encyclopedia of Terrorism*. He also nationalized, or took government control of, many resources, especially Libya's vast oil reserves, which, until then, had been operated by Western oil companies. He led the way when numerous Middle Eastern countries decided to form the Organization of the Petroleum Exporting Companies (OPEC) to control the price and production of oil and increase Middle Eastern leverage on Western powers.

"Libya's oil wealth, compared with the country's small population, meant that Gaddafi could afford to carry out reforms at home while pursuing a range of foreign policies that normally would be beyond the scope of a small state," according to the *Historical Dictionary of Civil Wars in Africa*. The reforms at home included a quasi-Communistic redistribution of property, where workers would take over enterprises and landlords lost their property. "This immediately produced shortages and hoarding of basic commodities . . . and increased widespread economic inefficiency," wrote Lisa Anderson in the *Encyclopedia of the Modern Middle East and North Africa*. Again, only Libya's oil wealth staved off disaster.

In foreign policy, Gaddafi set himself against the West, which he saw as corrupt and exploitative. He used his resources to fund global terrorism on many fronts. He provided funds and arms to terrorist organizations from Armenia to Nicaragua and from Japan to the Philippines. Libya was involved in the funding of Palestinian terrorism and in Irish terrorism against Britain. "Libya has not only provided these groups with funds but also sent arms—in some cases tons of weaponry—and allowed them to establish training camps in the country," according to the *Encyclopedia of Terrorism*.

Besides funding foreign groups, Libya has been involved more directly in terrorist acts. One of the most notorious of these occurred in 1986, when Libyan intelligence operatives bombed a nightclub in Berlin, killing two American servicemen and wounding hundreds of others. As a direct result of this attack, President Ronald Reagan, who famously called Gaddafi "the mad dog of the Middle East," ordered missile strikes on Libya. The strikes killed numerous civilians, as well as Gaddafi's baby daughter.

Even more shocking than the nightclub bombing was the sabotage of a Pan Am jumbo jet flying from London to New York in 1988. A Libyan intelligence agent was eventually convicted and imprisoned for planting a bomb on the plane. The death toll included 259 passengers and eleven people on the ground in Lockerbie, Scotland, where the plane "crashed into a petrol station in the centre of town . . . and burst into a 300-foot fireball," according to a December 21, 2008, article on the BBC News website. Gaddafi was accused by high-ranking Libyan officials of personally ordering the bombing, though he himself denied direct involvement.

Afterwards, Gaddafi moved toward a less confrontational stance with the West. In the early 2000s, he renounced terrorism and ended his efforts to obtain materials for a nuclear bomb. His treatment of his own people remained oppressive, however, and in 2011 a wave of revolutions in Arab nations sparked a Libyan rebellion against his rule. Gaddafi's response was violent and uncompromising, and Libya descended into a civil war.

American and North Atlantic Treaty Organization (NATO) troops provided aid to rebel forces, and slowly Gaddafi and his supporters were forced to cede control of much of the country. On October 20, 2011, Gaddafi was captured and killed by rebel forces. His death marked the end of an erratic, often brutal, reign that had spanned more than forty years. His death was seen by many as a sign of broader changes in the Middle East in a period when many long-serving dictators had been forced from power. In an October 21, 2011, Reuters article by Sami Aboudi, a Beirut shopkeeper named Ziad Khalil was quoted as saying, "The world now has one less dictator. . . . This is the end he deserves."

The rest of this book looks at aspects of contemporary Libya in chapters titled What Is the Status of Human Rights Issues in Libya?, How Have WMDs and Terrorism Affected Libya's International Status?, What Issues Impact Libya's Resistance Movement?, and What Should the US Role in Libya Be? Different authors present various viewpoints on Libya's place in world affairs and on its future.

CHAPTER

What Is the Status of Human Rights Issues In Libya?

Chapter Preface

One of the most controversial instances of human rights abuses in Libya in recent years was the Abu Salim prison massacre. According to Human Rights Watch in a June 27, 2006, article, a mass killing occurred in Tripoli's (Libya's capital city) Abu Salim prison, run by the Internal Security Agency, in the summer of 1996. Inmates at the prison reportedly rioted to protest restricted family visits and poor living conditions. After the prisoners surrendered, security forces moved them into a courtyard and fired on them for more than an hour. In total, they killed "'around 1,200 people,'" according to an inmate interviewed by Human Rights Watch. This would have been the majority of the sixteen to seventeen hundred prisoners held in Abu Salim at the time.

Human Rights Watch's report was based on testimony from only one prisoner, and the Libyan government initially denied any killings had taken place. The son of Muammar Gaddafi, Saif al-Islam, however, finally ordered an investigation into the affair in 2009. He said that killings had occurred, partially as a result of a confrontation between government forces and radical Islamic militants known as the Libyan Islamic Fighting Group. Judge Mohammed Bashir al-Khadhar was appointed to investigate, declaring, "We need to clear up this question concerning Libya's past," according to a September 6, 2009, report by Ali Shuaib for Reuters.

Despite official promises, however, the Abu Salim massacre was never fully investigated nor explained. Families were not told for years whether their relatives were dead or alive; bodies were never released.

In fact, the government's intransigence about the massacre may have been part of the cause of the 2011 rebellion against Gaddafi's rule. "Over the last four years, the families [of those killed in the massacre] have demonstrated every Saturday demanding justice and answers," Lindsey Hilsum reported in the blog of Channel 4 News. On February 15, after their lawyer, Fathi Terbil, was arrested, they demonstrated again. Thousands more, inspired by other revolutions across the Middle East, joined them. According to Terbil,

> We, the Abu Salim families ignited the revolution. . . . The Libyan people were ready to rise up because of the injustice they experienced in their lives, but they needed a cause. So calling for the release of people, including me, who had been arrested became the justification for their protests.

The rest of this chapter looks at other human rights violations and issues in Libya.

"The Libyan Arab Jamahiriya believed that the promotion and protection of human rights was one of the most important factors for the progress and development of the people."

Libya Has Made Significant Progress in Human Rights

United Nations Human Rights Council

The Human Rights Council (HRC) is an intergovernmental body within the United Nations that is responsible for strengthening the promotion and protection of human rights around the globe. In the following viewpoint, which was not officially released, the HRC reports on a review of Libya's human rights record. Libya itself notes its progress in human rights, including freedom of expression, freedom of religion, and women's equality. Other nations on the council largely praise Libya for its progress in these areas and for its commitment to human rights.

As you read, consider the following questions:

1. According to the Libyan delegation, Libyan women occupy prominent positions in what areas?

2. Basic laws and the Great Green Charter of Human Rights of the Jamahiriyan Era state that religion is what, according to the Libyan delegation?

3. For what did Syria (the Syrian Arab Republic) praise Libya?

The Libyan Arab Jamahiriya [that is, Libya] stated that it highly valued the universal periodic review as one of the most important human rights mechanisms in the United Nations, in which all countries were equal. It was a neutral, nonselective mechanism, with no double standards.

Libya Supports Human Rights

The delegation noted that the national report had been prepared in a transparent and consultative manner. A national committee had been established with the participation of representatives from all relevant sectors. Consultations with civil society organizations and relevant stakeholders had also been held.

The Libyan Arab Jamahiriya believed that the promotion and protection of human rights was one of the most important factors for the progress and development of the people. The first declaration of the Great Al-Fateh Revolution in 1969 [in which Muammar Gaddafi came to power] had called for equality and non-discrimination, and in 1977 the People's Authority had been declared. In 1988, the Libyan Arab Jamahiriya had issued the Great Green Document on Human Rights [Great Green Charter of Human Rights of the Jamahiriyan Era], which provided that all human beings were born free and equal, with no difference between men and women. In 1991, Law No. 20 on Strengthening Freedoms had also been enacted. The Libyan Arab Jamahiriya was party to most human rights treaties and the protocols thereto, and those instruments took precedence over national laws and could be directly applied by the courts once they had been ratified.

The Libyan Arab Jamahiriya also referred to its interaction with the human rights special procedures. Recently, invitations had been addressed to the [United Nations] Special Rapporteur on the right to education and the Special Rapporteur on the sale of children, child prostitution and child pornography. The Libyan Arab Jamahiriya was awaiting their responses to those invitations. On 30 June 2010, the Libyan Arab Jamahiriya had also invited Amnesty International [an international human rights organization] to visit the country to see for itself that the Libyan Arab Jamahiriya had never forcibly evicted or discriminated against any member of the Toubou tribe.

The delegation noted that all rights and freedoms were contained in a coherent, consolidated legal framework. The legal guarantees formed the basis for protection of the basic rights of the people. Further, abuses that might occur were dealt with by the judiciary, and the perpetrators were brought before justice. The judiciary safeguarded the rights of individuals and was assisted by other entities, most importantly the Office of the Public Prosecutor. A National Human Rights Commission, with a mandate based on the Paris Principles, had also been established, in 2007. The aforementioned entities were complemented by newly established mechanisms, such as civil society organizations established under Law No. 19 of 2001.

Protection of human rights was guaranteed in the Libyan Arab Jamahiriya; this included not only political rights, but also economic, social and cultural rights. The Libyan Arab Jamahiriya referred to its pioneering experience in the field of wealth distribution and labour rights.

The delegation indicated that women were highly regarded in the Libyan Arab Jamahiriya, and their rights were guaranteed by all laws and legislation. Discriminatory laws had been revoked. Libyan women occupied prominent positions in the public sector, the judicial system, the public prosecutor's office, the police and the military. Libyan legislation also guaranteed children their rights, and provided for special care for children with special needs, the elderly and persons with disabilities.

Illegal immigration was one of the greatest challenges faced by the country. Illegal immigration had a negative impact on the State budget, development, health, environmental programmes and social stability. The Libyan Arab Jamahiriya looked forward to coordination and cooperation with concerned countries, particularly European countries of destination for migrants, to set up comprehensive programmes to address the economic and social roots of this phenomenon by helping immigrants to settle in their own countries, providing them with work opportunities and assisting their countries in development plans.

The Libyan Arab Jamahiriya believed that human rights education was a duty that should be fulfilled in the school system and the family system and by relevant civil society organizations.

Rights Guaranteed in Libya

The [Libyan] delegation provided responses to some of the questions asked in advance, indicating that it hoped that delegations would respect the religious, social and cultural specificities of the Libyan people.

The Libyan Arab Jamahiriya noted that laws safeguarded freedom of expression through principles enshrined in the Great Green Document. Article 5 promoted the right of expression of every person. This right had been enshrined in the Code on the Promotion of Freedom, which, in its article 8, stated that "each citizen has the right to express his opinions and ideas openly in People's Congresses and in all mass media, no citizen is questioned on the exercise of this right unless this has been abused in a way that prejudices the People's Authority or is used for personal interest, and it is prohibited to advocate ideas and opinions in a clandestine manner or to

Membership of the Human Rights Council
June 19, 2010–June 18, 2011— by Regional Groups

African States	Asian States	Eastern European States
Angola 2013	Bahrain 2011	Hungary 2012
Burkina Faso 2011	Bangladesh 2012	Poland 2013
Cameroon 2012	China 2012	Republic of
Djibouti 2012	Japan 2011	Moldova 2013
Gabon 2011	Jordan 2012	Russian
Ghana 2011	Kyrgyzstan 2012	Federation 2012
Libyan Arab	Malaysia 2013	Slovakia 2011
Jamahiriya 2013	Maldives 2013	Ukraine 2011
Mauritania 2013	Pakistan 2011	
Mauritius 2012	Qatar 2013	
Nigeria 2012	Republic of	
Senegal 2012	Korea 2011	
Uganda 2013	Saudi Arabia 2012	
Zambia 2011	Thailand 2013	

Latin American & Caribbean States	Western Europe & Other States
Argentina 2011	Belgium 2012
Brazil 2011	France 2011
Chile 2011	Norway 2012
Cuba 2012	Spain 2013
Ecuador 2013	Switzerland 2013
Guatemala 2013	United Kingdom 2011
Mexico 2012	United States 2012
Uruguay 2012	

NOTE: Members are elected to staggered three-year terms. The year after each name shows when the term expires.

TAKEN FROM: UN Human Rights Council, "Membership of the Human Rights Council 19 June 2010–18 June 2011—by Regional Groups," 2011. www2.ohchr.org.

seek to disseminate them through force, temptation or terrorism". Additionally, it was a basic law with which all contradictory or conflicting legislation should be compatible and was to be amended accordingly. In the context of freedom of expression, each citizen, male or female, who had reached the age of 18 was entitled to membership in the Basic People's Congresses and, by virtue of that membership, had the right to express his or her opinion on any matter. Further, in view of the growth of information networks, restrictions imposed on freedom of expression had become an obsolete issue and such freedom could be prevented. With regarding to revoking legislation that restricted freedom of expression, the Libyan Arab Jamahiriya indicated that such legislation does not exist and that Libyan basic law explicitly mentioned freedom of expression.

Freedom of religion was also guaranteed, in accordance with basic laws and the Green Document, which stipulated that religion was a private spiritual and individual value and constituted a direct relationship with the Creator (God).

Regarding measures taken to prevent torture and ill treatment in detention centres or prisons, the Libyan Arab Jamahiriya indicated that the practice of torture and ill treatment was forbidden in article 434 of the Penal Code, which stated that public officials who had ordered the torture of a person or had committed an act of torture were sentenced to 3 to 10 years' imprisonment. Article 17 of the Promotion of Freedom Act stipulated that society forbade penalties that undermined the dignity of a person and inflicted physical harm or material injury. The legislation adequately addressed this issue; therefore, new measures were unnecessary in this context.

People who had been harmed could file a complaint with the general prosecutor. The public prosecutor's office periodically inspected police and prison centres during unannounced visits. From 1 January 2009 until 30 June 2010, the prosecutor had dealt with 7 cases involving torture and 66 cases involving the withholding of liberty. This showed that these were individual cases and that the issue did not constitute a national phenomenon.

Regarding extending invitations to special procedures, the Libyan Arab Jamahiriya reaffirmed its cooperation with these procedures, provided that mandate holders abided by the Code of Conduct governing their work, that they respected the mandate entrusted to them by the Council and that they did not interfere in the internal affairs of the State. The Libyan Arab Jamahiriya had extended invitations to the Special Rapporteur on the right to education and the Special Rapporteur on the sale of children, prostitution and [child] pornography.

With regard to the extent of consultation with civil society in the preparation of the national report, as indicated earlier, the Libyan Arab Jamahiriya noted that a Committee had been established to include all human rights authorities in addressing this matter.

Progress on Prison, Media, and Other Issues

Concerning the question of the presence of independent national human rights institutions, numerous human rights organizations had been established under Act No. 19/2001, including, most notably, the Wa'itasimo foundation, the [Gaddafi] International Charity and Development Foundation.

Regarding the amendment introduced in the Civil and Press Codes, a new bill that would regulate mass media in a comprehensive manner was envisaged. Some media representatives, particularly journalists, had suggested that the bill should be further examined by relevant media unions, owners of newspapers and independent broadcasts so that it could achieve its intended goal. In the Civil Code, the texts concerning commercial activities and branches had been regulated under Act No. 23 of 2010. Concerning civil issues, a partial amendment to the matter that required legal improvements was currently under consideration by the General People's Committee.

Concerning progress in the investigations into the disturbances of the Abu Salim prison [in 1996, human rights organizations said more than twelve hundred prisoners were murdered in the prison], the investigations were being carried out by a judge of the High Court assigned to do so by the General Assembly of the Supreme Court. Work was still in progress, and the National Human Rights Committee was awaiting the results of the investigations. Persons and their relatives involved in this issue had entered into negotiations, in accordance with social traditions, and some had been provided with financial reparations for damages, remaining cases had been brought before the courts.

With regard to the release of all political prisoners, those who had abandoned the use of terrorist acts had been released.

Regarding the granting of nationality to children born by Libyan women married to foreigners, Code No. 24 of 2010, granting such children the right to acquire Libyan nationality, was currently in the process of being published.

With respect to the country's strategy for dealing with illegal immigration, it was based on two points: first, urging concerted international efforts, and secondly, legislative action provided for in Law No. 19/2010 on illegal immigration, imposing rigid penalties on those who had transferred or prepared false documents for illegal immigrants.

Regarding the steps taken to implement the 2009 recommendations of the Committee on the Elimination of Discrimination against Women, the Libyan Arab Jamahiriya was scheduled to provide responses to the observations in the periodic report due in 2014. Some steps had been taken already, such as the establishment of a joint committee, including the Secretariat of Women Affairs of the General People's Congress, the National Planning Council and the General People's Committee for Social Affairs, to develop a working strategy for promoting the political, economic and social empowerment of women. An agreement had been reached between the representative of the United Nations Development Programme in the Libyan Arab Jamahiriya and the Women's Affairs Secretariat with a view to cooperation with the United Nations country team.

Response of Other States

Algeria noted the efforts of the Libyan Arab Jamahiriya to promote human rights, which reflected the country's commitment to complying with Human Rights Council resolutions and cooperating with the international community. Algeria welcomed the national institutional framework that had been set up, in particular the National Human Rights Committee. It noted that the country had made some progress in the area of education, as well as social and economic progress since the lifting of economic sanctions. It also noted the challenge of increased illegal immigration. Algeria made recommendations.

Qatar praised the legal framework for the protection of human rights and freedoms, including, inter alia [among other things], its criminal code and criminal procedure law, which provided legal guarantees for the implementation of those rights. Qatar expressed appreciation for the improvements made in the areas of education and health care, the rights of women, children and the elderly, and the situation of people with special needs. Qatar inquired about measures to tackle illegal immigration. Qatar made a recommendation.

The Sudan inquired if the Libyan Arab Jamahiriya could provide it with information about the initiative to distribute wealth to low-income families and whether the country considered this to be the best means to improve the standard of living of families with limited resources. It noted the country's positive experience in achieving a high school enrolment rate and improvements in the education of women. The Sudan made recommendations.

The Syrian Arab Republic praised the Libyan Arab Jamahiriya for its serious commitment to and interaction with the Human Rights Council and its mechanisms. It commended the country for its democratic regime based on promoting the people's authority through the holding of public conferences, which enhanced development and respect for human rights, while respecting cultural and religious traditions. It asked about the social care system for the elderly and the living conditions at their special homes. The Syrian Arab Republic made a recommendation.

The Democratic People's Republic of Korea [North Korea] praised the Libyan Arab Jamahiriya for its achievements in the protection of human rights, especially in the field of economic and social rights, including income augmentation, social care, a free education system, increased delivery of health care services, care for people with disabilities, and efforts to empower women. It noted the functioning of the constitutional and legislative framework and national entities. The Democratic People's Republic of Korea made recommendations.

Bahrain noted that the Libyan Arab Jamahiriya had adopted various policies aimed at improving human rights, in particular the right to education and the rights of persons with disabilities. Bahrain commended the free education system and praised programmes such as electronic examinations and teacher training. It commended the country for its efforts regarding persons with disabilities, particularly all the services and rehabilitation programmes provided. Bahrain made a recommendation.

Palestine commended the Libyan Arab Jamahiriya for the consultations held with civil society in the preparation of the national report, which demonstrated its commitment to the improved enjoyment of human rights. Palestine praised the country for the Great Green Document on Human Rights. It noted the establishment of the national independent institution entrusted with promoting and protecting human rights, which had many of the competencies set out in the Paris Principles. It also noted the interaction of the Libyan Arab Jamahiriya with human rights mechanisms.

Iraq commended the Libyan Arab Jamahiriya for being a party to most international and regional human rights instruments, which took precedence over its national legislation. It welcomed the efforts to present a comprehensive overview of the human rights situation in the country based on the unity among democracy, development and human rights. It also commended the Libyan Arab Jamahiriya for its cooperation with the international community. Iraq made recommendations.

Saudi Arabia commended the Libyan Arab Jamahiriya's achievements in its constitutional, legislative and institutional frameworks, which showed the importance that the country attached to human rights, and for the fact that international treaties took precedence over its national legislation. It noted that the Libyan Arab Jamahiriya had become party to many human rights conventions and had equipped itself with a number of institutions, national, governmental and nongovernmental, tasked with promoting and protecting human rights. Saudi Arabia made a recommendation.

"Citizens did not have the right to change their government. Continuing problems included reported disappearances; torture; arbitrary arrest; . . . and poor prison conditions."

Libya's Human Rights Record Remains Poor

US Department of State

The US Department of State is the cabinet-level department of the US government responsible for foreign affairs. In the following viewpoint, the State Department argues that Libya's human rights record is poor. Though Libyans are guaranteed political rights on paper, in practice the people have no say in the government and are denied freedom of expression, freedom of assembly, and other rights. The State Department also says that the justice system is inequitable and that women face discrimination and oppression in Libya.

As you read, consider the following questions:

1. What were some of the methods of torture reported in Libya during previous years, according to the report?

US Department of State, "2009 Human Rights Report: Libya," March 11, 2010. http://www.state.gov.

2. What does the report say the Libyan government did to all privately owned media?

3. What does the *Green Book* say is the basis of the political system, and how accurate is this statement?

The Great Socialist People's Libyan Arab Jamahiriya [Libya] is an authoritarian regime with a population of approximately 6.3 million, ruled by Colonel Mu'ammar al-Qadhafi since 1969. The country's governing principles are derived predominantly from al-Qadhafi's *Green Book* ideology. In theory citizens rule the country through a pyramid of popular congresses, communes, and committees, as laid out in the 1969 Constitutional Proclamation and the 1977 Declaration on the Establishment of the Authority of the People. After elections in March [2009], Secretary of the General People's Committee al-Baghdadi al-Mahmoudi (prime minister equivalent) and the delegates of the 760-member General People's Congress began three-year terms. In practice al-Qadhafi and his inner circle monopolized political power. These authorities generally maintained effective control of the security forces.

A Poor Record

The government's human rights record remained poor. Citizens did not have the right to change their government. Continuing problems included reported disappearances; torture; arbitrary arrest; lengthy pretrial and sometimes incommunicado detention; official impunity; and poor prison conditions. Denial of fair public trial by an independent judiciary, political prisoners and detainees, and the lack of judicial recourse for alleged human rights violations were also problems. The government instituted new restrictions on media freedom and continued to restrict freedom of speech (including Internet and academic freedom). It continued to impede the freedom of assembly, freedom of association, and civil liberties. The government did not fully protect the rights of migrants, asylum seekers, and refugees, and in some cases participated in their abuse. Other problems included restrictions on freedom of religion; corruption and lack of transparency; discrimination against women, ethnic minorities, and foreign workers; trafficking in persons; and restriction of labor rights.

Respect for the Integrity of the Person, Including Freedom From:

a. Arbitrary or Unlawful Deprivation of Life

There were no confirmed reports that the government or its agents committed arbitrary or unlawful killings. On May 10 [2009], the Tripoli [Libyan capital] newspaper *Oea* reported that Ali al-Fakheri (also known as Ibn al-Shaykh al-Libi) had been found dead in his cell in Abu Salim prison from an apparent suicide, and that the General Prosecutor's Office (GPO) had begun an investigation. The nongovernmental organization (NGO) Human Rights Watch (HRW) had met briefly with al-Fakheri during a visit to the prison on April 27, but he refused to be interviewed. In a May 12 statement, HRW called on authorities to conduct a full and transparent investigation. The NGO Amnesty International (AI) visited Abu Salim prison after his death in May, but authorities denied access to al-Fakheri's guards, forensic doctors, or the autopsy report. There were no results of the GPO investigation made public by year's end.

On August 31, the NGO Committee to Protect Journalists (CPJ) called for a credible and transparent inquiry into the reported 2007 trial and sentencing to death of three unnamed individuals for the 2005 killing of Daif al-Ghazal, a prominent opposition journalist and anticorruption activist.

There were no developments in the case of Mohamed Adel Abu Ali, who died in custody in May 2008 after his return to the country when his asylum claim was denied in Europe. According to HRW, he was tortured in detention. London-based

Aharq Al-Awsat reported that he belonged to the oppositionist "al-Tabu" Front for the Liberation of Libya.

b. Disappearance

In 2007 security services arrested Abdulrahman al-Qutiwi, along with others who appeared subsequently in court to face criminal charges. Authorities did not bring al-Qutiwi to trial. After two years of incommunicado detention during which his whereabouts were unknown, authorities released al-Qutiwi in mid-February.

Torture

c. Torture and Other Cruel, Inhuman, or Degrading Treatment or Punishment

The law prohibits such practices, but security personnel reportedly routinely tortured and abused detainees and prisoners during interrogations or as punishment. Detainees often were held incommunicado. Foreign observers noted that incidents of torture—used as a punishment in Internal Security Service prisons—seemed to have decreased over the past year.

There were reports of torture and abuse during the year. On December 10, the Qadhafi Development Foundation (QDF) released a report on human rights practices in the country. In a statement accompanying the release, the QDF said during the year it had received a "large number of complaints" of torture during imprisonment and called for the government to waive immunities from prosecution for officials accused of torture. The Human Rights Society of Libya (HRSL), the QDF subsidiary responsible for the report, noted that suspected narcotraffickers were among those most mistreated, with punishments including beating with sticks. On March 9, International Christian Concern, an NGO dedicated to religious issues, alleged that four converts to Christianity, arrested in January, had been physically abused in detention, although no specific methods or further details were provided. According to a June 9 HRW report, migrants in Malta and

Italy previously apprehended in Libya reported that authorities severely abused them. On May 20, HRW interviewed an Eritrean migrant in Rome who alleged officials in Libya beat him with sticks and metal rods at a migrant detention facility. On September 15, Algeria's human rights commissioner stated that 26 of 54 Algerian prisoners released from prisons in the country as part of an annual Revolution Day amnesty "suffered from the effects of torture."

In previous years the reported methods of torture and abuse included chaining prisoners to a wall for hours; clubbing; applying electric shock; applying corkscrews to the back; pouring lemon juice in open wounds; breaking fingers and allowing the joints to heal without medical care; suffocating with plastic bags; depriving detainees of sleep, food, and water; hanging by the wrists; suspending from a pole inserted between the knees and elbows; burning with cigarettes; threatening with dog attacks; and beatings on the soles of the feet.

The law sanctioned corporal punishments such as amputation and flogging, although there were no reports that such punishments were carried out.

No further information was available at year's end concerning the June 2008 alleged abduction, interrogation, and torture of lawyer Dhaw al-Mansuri.

In July 2008 Saif al-Islam al-Qadhafi, son of Colonel Mu'ammar al-Qadhafi, conceded that acts of torture and excessive violence had taken place in prisons. Al-Qadhafi denied government culpability, arguing that the individuals responsible for the torture had acted on their own initiative and were being tried within the legal system. At year's end there was no information released on the progress of trials.

On April 19, Ashraf Ahmad Jum'a al-Hajuj drew attention to his suit against the Libyan government at a preparatory meeting for the Durban Review Conference, chaired by Libyan diplomat Najat al-Hajjaji. Al-Hajuj, a Palestinian doctor, was arrested in 1999 on charges that he and five Bulgarian nurses working in Benghazi infected hundreds of children. In January 2008 he filed suit in France and at the UN Human Rights Commission in Geneva, arguing he was tortured repeatedly in detention. According to his testimony, the torture included rape by a German shepherd, fingernails ripped off, and electric shocks. He also testified that he was present when the Bulgarian nurses detained with him were tortured. He said most of the torture occurred during the early period after his imprisonment in 1999. At year's end the case was awaiting further action in a French court. . . .

Civil Liberties

Respect for Civil Liberties, Including:

a. Freedom of Speech and Press

The law provides for freedom of speech "within the limits of public interest and principles of the Revolution," but in practice the Publication Act of 1972 severely limits the freedoms of speech and of the press, particularly criticism of government officials or policy. The government tolerated some difference of opinion within governmental structures in people's committee meetings and at the General People's Congress. HRW met with a group of journalists during an April [2009] visit to the country. While the journalists acknowledged that restrictions on press freedoms had generally loosened over the past years, they lamented that new freedoms were based not in law but on "personalities" of those enforcing laws—including the Publication Act, which in practice allows the government to silence critics through slander and libel provisions.

The government prohibited all unofficial political activities. The law permits authorities to interpret many forms of speech or expression as illegal. The wide reach of security services and broad networks of informants resulted in pervasive self-censorship.

Human Rights in Libya Remain Erratic

Over the past decade [1999–2009] Libya dramatically transformed its international status from a pariah state under UN [United Nations], EU [European Union] and US sanctions to a country that, in 2009 alone, held the Presidency of the UN Security Council, the chair of the African Union and the Presidency of the UN General Assembly. But this transformation in Libya's foreign policy has not galvanized an equivalent transformation of Libya's human rights record which remains poor, despite some limited progress in recent years. . . .

Despite work to develop a new penal code, an essentially repressive legal framework remains in place, as does the ability of government security forces to act with impunity against dissent. Many trials, especially those before the State Security Court, still fail to meet international due process standards. Overall, unjustified limits on free expression and association remain the norm, including penal code provisions that criminalize "insulting public officials" or "opposing the ideology of the Revolution." Many relatives of prisoners killed in a 1996 incident at Abu Salim prison are still waiting to learn how their relatives died and to see those responsible punished. The jurisdiction of courts, the duties of government agencies, respect for legal rights of prisoners and adherence to the country's stated list of human rights often remain murky, erratic and contradictory.

Human Rights Watch,
Truth and Justice Can't Wait: Human Rights Developments in Libya Amid Institutional Obstacles, *2009, pp. 1–2.*

The government owned and controlled virtually all print and broadcast media. The official news agency, the Jamahiriya News Agency (JANA), is the designated conduit for official views. Government-controlled media neither published nor broadcast opinions inconsistent with official policy. In 2008 the quasi-official al-Ghad Media Group, a QDF subsidiary controlled by Saif al-Islam al-Qadhafi, launched a satellite television station, a radio station, and two independent newspapers. According to the NGO Reporters Without Borders, most of the journalists at these newspapers also work for official media outlets, and the newspapers were printed on the government's presses. Local revolutionary committees published several small newspapers.

During the year the government nationalized all privately owned news media, reversing the decision in 2007 to allow a few private media outlets. On April 24, the state-run al-Jamahiriya television feed interrupted quasi-independent al-Libiyya satellite television channel in the middle of an interview program. According to press reports, JANA officials took over al-Libiyya's offices and the station manager and deputy director of al-Ghad Media Group, Abdelsalam al-Mishri, was arrested and held for two days. On June 3, opposition websites reported General People's Committee decree 226 of 2009, placing the al-Ghad Media Group under state-run National Center for Media Services control. All news outlets under the group's umbrella continued to publish and broadcast through the end of the year, and Saif al-Islam announced that al-Libiyya would relocate to London or Jordan for business reasons. On August 20, al-Ghad-sponsored al-Mutawasit began original programming broadcasts from Jordan. Within days, however, its signal ran al-Jamahiriya feeds in simulcast. It had not resumed original programming at the end of the year.

On October 21, Mohammed al-Sareet reported on Jeel Libya, a London-based website, about a demonstration carried out by residents of a state-run care center for women that had been orphaned as children calling for the removal of the center's director for sexual harassment. On October 22, al-Sareet was reportedly questioned by police and subsequently charged with criminal defamation of the center's director. Quotations attributed in al-Sareet's original reporting were retracted by the women in subsequent coverage of the event, reportedly under pressure from government officials. On October 31, however, the General Prosecutor's Office charged the center's director with sexual harassment and reportedly dropped all charges against al-Sareet.

Some outlets in Tripoli had limited quantities of international weekly publications. Although the publications law in theory restricts publishing rights to public entities, private companies were able to distribute newspapers and books in practice.

Assembly

b. Freedom of Peaceful Assembly and Association

Freedom of Assembly

The law stipulates that "individuals may meet peacefully, and no police personnel are entitled to attend their meetings; moreover, they are not obliged to notify the police of such gatherings." The law also provides for the right to hold public meetings in accordance with the regulations set by law. In practice, however, the government severely restricted these rights and permitted public assembly only with express advance approval and only in support of its positions. Family groups of victims of the 1996 Abu Salim prison riots [in which more than twelve hundred prisoners were killed] who protested in Benghazi periodically throughout the year faced harassment, and authorities arrested four for their protests, according to foreign opposition groups.

Freedom of Association

The government restricted the right of association to institutions affiliated with the government. The government did not allow the formation of groups based on political ideology inconsistent with the 1969 revolution.

In its December 10 report and press conference in Tripoli, LHRS [Libyan Human Rights Solidarity] demanded that Law 19 of 1992 that restricts formation of civil society organizations be repealed and pressed for adoption of a new law—in draft since 2008—that would remove the ability of the state to suspend organizations without cause.

c. Freedom of Religion

Although there is no explicit law guaranteeing religious freedom, the government generally respected in practice the right to observe one's religion. Islam is the equivalent of a state religion and is thoroughly integrated into everyday political and social life.

The government regulated mosques, religious schools, and clerics to ensure that all views were in line with the state-approved form of Islam. The government strongly opposed militant forms of Islam, which it viewed as a threat to the regime.

The World Islamic Call Society (WICS), an international educational institution, operated a state-run university in Tripoli that provided Muslims from outside the Arab world with a broad education in literature, history, science, and religion. WICS also organized vocational training programs, offered students exposure to international academic speakers, and maintained relations with local non-Muslim religious groups, including Christian churches.

Although there is no law prohibiting conversion from Islam, the government prohibits efforts to proselytize Muslims and actively prosecutes offenders. International Christian Concern, a Christian rights NGO, reported that four citizen converts to Christianity were detained at a state security prison in Tripoli in January and allegedly held without charge in incommunicado detention for three months and interrogated, abused, and pressured to reveal the names of other converts. Two weeks before their release, the converts were reportedly transferred to a reform and rehabilitation prison where family members were permitted to visit them. They were released on

April 21. In May authorities released Daniel Baidoo, a Ghanaian national, after eight years in prison. According to press reports, Baidoo had been imprisoned for proselytizing after receiving Christian biblical tracts at a local post office. The government permitted Christian churches to operate freely but imposed a limit of one church per denomination per city and monitored religious services, including Islamic services, for evidence of political discourse.

A noncitizen female who marries a Muslim citizen is not required to convert to Islam, but a noncitizen male must convert to Islam to marry a Muslim woman. The government maintained the position that all citizens were Muslims. . . .

Political Rights

Respect for Political Rights: The Right of Citizens to Change Their Government

The country does not have a constitution, and citizens do not have the right to change their government by peaceful means. The country's governing principles stem from al-Qadhafi's *Green Book*, which combines Islamic ideals with elements of socialism and pan-Arabism. The *Green Book* states that direct popular rule is the basis of the political system and that citizens play a role in popular congresses; in practice, al-Qadhafi and his close associates monopolized every aspect of decision making in the government. . . .

Official Corruption and Government Transparency

Laws stipulating criminal penalties for official corruption are unclear and inconsistently applied. The Administration Monitoring Board is the government agency responsible for oversight of official activities and prevention of corrupt practices. Officials regularly engaged in corrupt practices with impunity. Government corruption coupled with favoritism based on family and tribal ties were perceived to be severe problems. Both contributed to government inefficiency.

The law does not provide for financial disclosure by public officials or public access to government information, and the government did not provide access in practice to citizens, pressure groups, or the media. The government did not publicly provide detailed planning or budget documents.

Governmental Attitude Regarding International and Non-governmental Investigation of Alleged Violations of Human Rights

The government prohibited the establishment of independent nongovernmental human rights organizations, although the quasigovernmental QDF routinely criticized the government's human rights practices. Restrictive laws that imposed imprisonment for forming or joining international organizations without government authorization forced individuals wishing to carry out human rights work to operate abroad. In May QDF facilitated AI's first fact-finding visit to the country since 2004. The QDF also facilitated HRW's visit in April, just more than a year after the group's last visit, but restricted their access to prisons. The QDF facilitated the December 12 launch of HRW's report from Tripoli, the first such event in Libya by an international human rights organization.

Associations engaging in unauthorized political activity were illegal. The Libyan Arab Human Rights Committee, a government body, did not release any public reports. HRSL, operating under the sponsorship of the semiofficial QDF, released a report on December 10 criticizing government policies restricting civil society, calling for the abolition of the state security court, drawing attention to human rights abuses, and demanding resolution of claims stemming from the 1996 Abu Salim riot.

Discrimination

Discrimination, Societal Abuses, and Trafficking in Persons

The law prohibits discrimination based on race, sex, religion, disability, or social status. The government did not enforce these prohibitions effectively, particularly with regard to women and minorities.

Women

The 1969 Constitutional Proclamation granted women equality under the law. In practice traditional attitudes and practices continued that discriminated against women. Sharia [Islamic law] governs inheritance, divorce, and the right to own property. The law does not distinguish between genders for crimes of domestic violence, rape, or sexual harassment. Women have societal restrictions on their movement even to local destinations.

The law prohibits domestic violence, but there was scant information on the penalties or on the extent of violence against women. There were 563 cases of rape reported in 2007; statistics were not disaggregated by gender. In 2008 courts heard more than 900 cases involving sex crimes. On January 29, members of the Committee on the Elimination of Discrimination Against Women criticized the government for not presenting data on violence against women. Prison terms of varying length were handed down to convicted rapists, according to a July 24 government response to the UN Human Rights Committee. Domestic abuse was rarely discussed publicly; HRW reported that students conducting a study on sexual violence in April found that victims were reticent to discuss their experiences due to fears of social stigmatization.

The law criminalizes rape. A convicted rapist must marry the victim, with her agreement, or serve a prison term of as long as 25 years.

The law does not distinguish between rape and spousal rape. According to government officials responding to the UN Human Rights Committee, "if a wife is raped by force or in a way that she does not accept, she may lodge a complaint and demand that her husband be prosecuted and punished." There were 20 Women's Courts in Tripoli and in Benghazi to deal with cases that, according to government officials, could not be resolved privately and where women could avoid the social stigma of appearing in court alongside violent criminals.

The law prohibits prostitution, but there were reports that it existed in major cities.

The law does not prohibit female genital mutilation (FGM), which is foreign to the culture and society. There were no reports of FGM during the year.

Women and girls suspected of violating moral codes were detained indefinitely without being convicted or after having served a sentence and without the right to challenge their detention before a court. . . . They were held in "social rehabilitation" facilities, in some cases because they had been raped and then ostracized by their families. The government stated that a woman was free to leave a rehabilitation home when she reached "legal age" (18 years), consented to marriage, or was taken into the custody of a male relative. According to HRW, authorities transferred most women to these facilities against their will, and those who came of their own volition did so because no genuine shelters for survivors of violence exist. HRW maintained that the government routinely violated women's and girls' human rights in "social rehabilitation" homes, including violations of due process, freedom of movement, personal dignity, and privacy. One example of these violations is the practice of "virginity exams" in "social rehabilitation" facilities. According to a 2006 HRW report, medical providers conducted invasive examinations to determine whether women detained in "social rehabilitation" facilities had engaged in sexual intercourse. HRW notes that these exams have "no medical accuracy."

> "The group did not say whether it regretted mounting . . . a behind-the-scenes [public relations] campaign that snared prominent intellectuals hoping for the best in Libya."

Libya Has Paid Academics to Deliberately Whitewash Its Human Rights Record

David Corn and Siddhartha Mahanta

David Corn is Washington bureau chief for Mother Jones; *Siddhartha Mahanta is an editorial fellow at* Mother Jones. *In the following viewpoint, they report that Libya paid the management consulting firm the Monitor Group to improve its public image. They say that the Monitor Group paid intellectuals and academics to go to Libya and write articles portraying Libya and dictator Muammar Gaddafi in a positive light. Often, the authors say, these articles were published without adequately disclosing links to the Monitor Group.*

As you read, consider the following questions:

1. Who do the authors say obtained internal documents about the Monitor Group, and what did these documents reveal about the group's relationship with Libya?

2. What book was the Monitor Group supposed to produce for Libya, and how much were they to be paid?

3. Why did Robert Putnam say that he declined to make a second trip to Libya when asked to do so by the Monitor Group?

In February 2007 Harvard professor Joseph Nye Jr., who developed the concept of "soft power," visited Libya and sipped tea for three hours with Muammar Qaddafi. Months later, he penned an elegant description of the chat for the *New Republic*, reporting that Qaddafi had been interested in discussing "direct democracy." Nye noted that "there is no doubt that" the Libyan autocrat "acts differently on the world stage today than he did in decades past. And the fact that he took so much time to discuss ideas—including soft power—with a visiting professor suggests that he is actively seeking a new strategy." The article struck a hopeful tone: that there was a new Qaddafi. It also noted that Nye had gone to Libya "at the invitation of the Monitor Group, a consulting company that is helping Libya open itself to the global economy."

In Qaddafi's Pay

Nye did not disclose all. He had actually traveled to Tripoli as a paid consultant of the Monitor Group (a relationship he disclosed in an e-mail to *Mother Jones*), and the firm was working under a $3 million-per-year contract with Libya. Monitor, a Boston-based consulting firm with ties to the Harvard Business School, had been retained, according to internal documents obtained by a Libyan dissident group, not to promote economic development, but "to enhance the profile of

Libya and Muammar Qadhafi." So the *New Republic* published an article sympathetic to Qaddafi that had been written by a prominent American intellectual paid by a firm that was being compensated by Libya to burnish the dictator's image.

Presumably, Nye was sharing his independently derived view of Qaddafi. Yet a source familiar with the Harvard professor's original submission to the magazine notes, "It took considerable prodding from editors to get him to reluctantly acknowledge the regime's very well-known dark side." And Franklin Foer, then the editor of the magazine, says, "If we had known that he was consulting for a firm paid by the government, we wouldn't have run the piece." (After an inquiry by *Mother Jones*, the *New Republic* added a disclaimer to the Nye story acknowledging the details of Nye's relationship with Monitor.)

The Nye article was but one PR [public relations] coup the Monitor Group delivered for Qaddafi. But the firm also succeeded on other fronts. The two chief goals of the project, according to an internal document describing Monitor's Libya operations, were to produce a makeover for Libya and to introduce Qaddafi "as a thinker and intellectual, independent of his more widely-known and very public persona as the Leader of the Revolution in Libya." In a July 3, 2006, letter to its contact in the Libyan government, Mark Fuller, the CEO of Monitor, and Rajeev Singh-Molares, a director of the firm, wrote,

> Libya has suffered from a deficit of positive public relations and adequate contact with a wide range of opinion-leaders and contemporary thinkers. This program aims to redress the balance in Libya's favor.

Libyan Makeover

The key strategy for achieving these aims, the operation summary said, "involves introducing to Libya important international figures that will influence other nations' policies towards the country." Also on the table, according to a Monitor document was a book that Monitor would produce on "Qadhafi, the Man and His Ideas," based in part on interviews between the Libyan dictator and these visiting international influentials. The book supposedly would "enable the international intellectual and policy-making elite to understand Qadhafi as an individual thinker rather than leader of a state." (Monitor's fee for this particular task: $1.65 million.) This volume never materialized. But one primary outcome of Monitor's pro-Qaddafi endeavors, the operation summary said, was an increase in media coverage "broadly positive and increasingly sensitive to the Libyan point of view."

It worked: Several thought-leaders were brought to Libya by Monitor to chat with the leader—including neoconservative Richard Perle (who then briefed Vice President Dick Cheney on his visits), political economist Francis Fukuyama, and conservative scholar Bernard Lewis (who briefed the US embassy in Israel on his trip)—and a few of the "visitors," as Monitor referred to them, did write mostly positive articles, without revealing they had been part of the Monitor Group's endeavor to clean up Qaddafi. Some might not have even known they had been recruited for an image rehabilitation effort.

In 2006 and 2007, Benjamin [R.] Barber, an author specializing in democracy studies and a senior fellow at Demos, a pro-democracy think tank, took three trips to Libya as a paid consultant to Monitor. On these visits, Barber met with Libyan lawyers, officials, and activists interested in democratic reform—and Qaddafi, too. "We went," he says, "in the hope we might be able to reinforce elements inside Libya interested in change, looking to engage civil society and create a foundation for a movement." Barber served on the international advisory board of Qaddafi International Charity and Development Foundation, which was overseen by Saif Qaddafi, the second-eldest son of the Libyan dictator, who supported the foundation's work on human rights and democracy-promotion projects and who seemed a reformist himself (until last month [February 2011], when he sided with his father in declaring war on the protesters). "Did I realize that I was working within an autocratic regime and the odds of making change were low?" Barber remarks. "Yes."

Joseph Nye Objects

After this piece was posted, [Joseph] Nye complained to [Franklin] Foer about Foer's characterization of Nye's disclosure [in Nye's article in the *New Republic*]. Following that, Foer submitted this statement to *Mother Jones* [where this piece first ran]:

> Joseph Nye has just found the draft of the piece he submitted to the *New Republic*. In that draft he wrote, "I was in Libya at the invitation of a former Harvard colleague who works for the Monitor Group, a consulting company which has undertaken to help Libya open itself to the global economy. Part of that process is meeting with a variety of Western experts whom Monitor hires as consultants." Based on that information, TNR [the *New Republic*] should have prodded him to include a more explicit disclosure in the final version of his piece. Re-reading that draft, it's clear that my quote to you was far too categorical.

In an e-mail to *Mother Jones*, Nye wrote,

> I answered your questions honestly about whether I had been paid by Monitor, but you then wrote something different that was not true. You . . . accepted one source about whether I told TNR that I had been paid by Monitor without checking back with me. I attach the July [2007] draft of the article that I submitted to TNR. You will see that on line 9 I said that the consultants had been "hired" by Monitor. Hired means paid.

Nye did include a reference to paid consultants in his original draft, but this was not a clear statement that he had been paid directly by Monitor—and it certainly wasn't a disclosure that he had been paid as part of a Monitor project designed to clean up Qaddafi's image. Moreover, according to TNR editors, Nye didn't object to the final version of the *New Republic* piece, which, after extensive editing, no longer included a mention of Monitor paying outside consultants to engage in "meetings" in Libya. Asked whether he had objected to the final version, Nye told *Mother Jones*, "All I know is that I alerted them that I was paid."

The Purpose of Monitor

Barber says he believed that the main aim of the Monitor Group's Libya project was to stir reform there—trying to "turn Libya from a rogue state into a better state." He was encouraged by small steps he saw in the country. And in August 2007, Barber wrote an op-ed for the *Washington Post*, noting that Libya had finally released five Bulgarian nurses and a Palestinian doctor who each had been condemned to death for allegedly infecting children in a Libyan hospital with HIV. In the article—headlined "Gaddafi's Libya: An Ally for America?"—Barber wrote that his one-on-one conversations with Qaddafi had convinced him that the Libyan leader had arranged for their release to show his desire for "a genuine rapprochement with the United States."

"Libya," Barber noted, "under Gaddafi has embarked on a journey that could make it the first Arab state to transition peacefully and without overt Western intervention to a stable, non-autocratic government." He reported that Qaddafi, whom the United States and other governments had identified as a possible ally in the war against al Qaeda [the terrorist group that attacked the United States on September 11, 2001], had been "holding open conversations" with Western intellectuals.

But Barber did not mention in the *Post* piece that he himself had been a paid consultant for the Monitor Group. Was this an oversight? "I don't think so," Barber says, adding that he assumed he was on the payroll to help Monitor promote reform in Libya, not sell Qaddafi in the United States. (According to a blog post he wrote for the *Huffington Post* on February 22 [2011], Barber and all the members of the international advisory board of the Qaddafi foundation resigned in response to the Qaddafi's regime's violent reaction to the uprising in Libya.)

Other intellectuals squired to Libya by Monitor also chronicled their experiences in articles that bolstered the notion—for which there was a true basis at the time—that Qaddafi was heading in a positive direction. After being escorted to Libya by Monitor in 2007, Princeton University professor Andrew Moravcsik (who did not meet with the Libyan leader) contributed a long article to *Newsweek International*—"A Rogue Reforms"—that concluded, "Kaddafi may have no desire to surrender power himself—but he has come to see that embracing modernization and globalization is the best way to assure his survival. Thus the historical irony: after three decades of isolation, Libya may be emerging as the West's best hope in the turbulent Middle East." Asked about his trip to Libya and his relationship with Monitor—and whether he should have disclosed any connection in the *Newsweek* article—Moravcsik initially refused to comment; a spokeswoman for him said, "He is not available to discuss this issue." But this spokeswoman subsequently said that Moravcsik was not paid by the Monitor Group.

Anthony Giddens, a leading British intellectual, made two Monitor-guided trips to Libya in 2007. According to Monitor documents, he published two articles about Libya after each trip. In one of those pieces—"My chat with the colonel," posted by the *Guardian*—Giddens noted, "As one-party states go, Libya is not especially repressive. Gadafy seems genuinely popular." He observed, "Will real progress be possible only when Gadafy leaves the scene? I tend to think the opposite. If he is sincere in wanting change, as I think he is, he could play a role in muting conflict that might otherwise arise as modernisation takes hold." The article did not mention the Monitor Group. (A Monitor document notes, "Giddens regularly plays tennis with George Soros, and they are known to have discussed Libya a number of times.") Giddens did not respond to an e-mail request for comment.

Harvard professor Robert Putnam also traveled to Libya in 2007 under the auspices of the Monitor Group and spent several hours with Qaddafi in his tent in the desert. He, too, wrote about this experience—but not until last week, after the Libyan uprising had begun. In an article for the *Wall Street Journal*—"With Libya's Megalomaniac 'Philosopher-King'"—Putnam disclosed that "an international consulting firm that was advising the Libyan government on economic and political reform" had asked whether he would go to Libya and discuss his research on civil society and democracy with Qaddafi. He noted that "my hosts were willing to pay my standard consulting fee." In Libya, Putnam recounted, he spent two hours talking political philosophy with Qaddafi, who dismissed Putnam's celebration of civic groups and freedom of association, noting that adopting any of this in Libya could cause profound disunity.

A Public Relations Stunt

Putnam wrote,

> Was this a serious conversation or an elaborate farce? Naturally, I came away thinking—hoping—that I had managed to sway Col. Gadhafi in some small way, but my wife was skeptical. Two months later I was invited back to a public roundtable in Libya, but by then I had concluded that the whole exercise was a public relations stunt, and I declined.

In a statement, Monitor contends that its Libya project, which ended in 2008, "focused on helping the Libyan people work towards an improved economy and more open governmental institutions" and "was undertaken during a period that was widely perceived as holding meaningful potential for reform within, and new opportunity for, Libya." Indeed, at that point, a measure of reform in Libya appeared possible. But, according to Monitor's agreement with Libya, its project was more about peddling Qaddafi overseas than pitching reform to Qaddafi. Were Monitor officials slyly using the opportunity to enhance Qaddafi's image as a chance to promote change within his autocratic regime? (Or is that too charitable?) Monitor did not reply to questions from *Mother Jones* about its intentions in Libya, about its payments to consultants, or about the various articles that were written by the academics it brought to Tripoli.

"We do not discuss specifics of our work with any client," the Monitor statement says. "That said, we are deeply distressed and saddened to witness the current tragic events in Libya." The group did not say whether it regretted mounting, on behalf of a brutal dictator who proved to be no reformer, a behind-the-scenes PR campaign that snared prominent intellectuals hoping for the best in Libya.

> *"Libya is trying to impose an information blackout, but it can't hide a massacre."*

Libya's Attacks on Civilians Are a Violation of Human Rights

Human Rights Watch

Human Rights Watch (HRW) is an international human rights organization. In the following viewpoint, HRW reports that Libyan government forces have opened fire on peaceful protestors, killing more than two hundred people over several days. HRW also says that Libya has unlawfully arrested activists and closed down the Internet. HRW says that the international community must demand an end to the killing, impose embargoes on export of arms and security equipment to Libya, and work to hold those responsible for the shootings to account.

As you read, consider the following questions:

1. According to HRW, what has Libya done to make it difficult to obtain information on developments in the country?

2. How many protestors does HRW say were on the streets of Benghazi on February 20, 2011?

3. Who is Abdul Hafiz Ghogha, as explained by HRW?

The African Union and African, Western, and Arab countries that have relations with Libya should urge the Libyan government to stop the unlawful killing of protesters, Human Rights Watch said today [February 20, 2011]. In the last three, days the death toll of protesters reported to Human Rights Watch by hospital staff and other sources has reached at least 173.

Accounts of the use of live ammunition by security forces, including machine-gun fire, against protesters near the Katiba [a garrison] in Benghazi on February 19, 2011, resulting in dozens of deaths and injuries, raise serious concern that the authorities are using unjustified and unlawful force. The government has shut down all Internet communications in the country, and arrested Libyans who have given phone interviews to the media, making it extremely difficult to obtain information on developments there.

"A potential human rights catastrophe is unfolding in Libya as protesters brave live gunfire and death for a third day running," said Sarah Leah Whitson, Middle East and North Africa director at Human Rights Watch. "Libya is trying to impose an information blackout, but it can't hide a massacre."

Eyewitnesses told Human Rights Watch that at least 10,000 protesters are protesting in the streets of Benghazi on February 20, after the funerals of the 84 protesters shot dead the day before.

According to witnesses who spoke to Human Rights Watch, the violence started on February 19 after thousands of protesters had gathered for funeral prayers of 14 of the protesters shot dead by security forces the day before. Followed by thousands of protesters, the funeral procession walked from the square in front of the Benghazi court to the Hawaii cemeter-

Gadhafi Threatens Protestors and Rebels

They [those opposed to Gadhafi's regime] don't want me, they don't want Libya. This is the criminal act. Anybody who lifts an arm, any Libyan who lifts an arm shall be punished with death sentence. Those who spy with other countries shall be punished with death sentence. Anybody who undermines the sovereignty of the state shall be punished with death. . . .

. . . and when they are caught and prosecuted they will be begging for mercy, and this time we will not be so merciful, we will not be forgiving. Any who undermines the constitution, anyone, by force, or otherwise, to undermine and change by force or any other way, and the punishment is death. Any who use explosives shall be punished with death. . . .

Any use of force against the authority of the state, anyone causing murder shall be handed the death sentence.

BFW News,
"Gadhafi's 'Crazy' Speech Transcript,"
February 27, 2011. www.beyondthefirstworld.com.

ies. On the way the marchers passed the Katiba El Fadil Bu Omar, a complex that includes one of Colonel Muammar Gaddafi's residences and is heavily guarded by state security officers.

Firing on Civilians

Three eyewitnesses confirmed that the security officers in distinctive uniform with yellow berets fired indiscriminately on protesters. One protester, A.G., told Human Rights Watch, "it was at this stage that they opened fire on us. We were walking along peacefully but were chanting angrily against the regime and Gaddafi."

Another lawyer who was at the protests said to Human Rights Watch, "I could see the men with yellow berets shooting at us with live gunfire, and dozens fell to the ground. This went on for a long period of time, and I left with the injured to the hospital." Later in the afternoon, Human Rights Watch spoke to another protester who said he had left the area because "anyone who goes near the Katiba is shot." In the evening, thousands of protesters were still gathered in front of the Benghazi courthouse.

Human Rights Watch spoke to a senior medical official at al-Jalaa hospital in Beghazi who said the dead started coming in at 3:00 p.m. and that by the end of the day, he had received 23 bodies. By the morning of February 20, the number of dead who arrived at the hospital had risen to 70. He said the deaths and the vast majority of those injured showed gunshot wounds of 4cm x 4cm sustained to the head, neck, and shoulders. Medical officials at Hawaii hospital in Benghazi told Human Rights Watch that they had received 14 bodies. Human Rights Watch also confirmed the death of at least one protester in Misrata on February 19, bringing the total number of those killed on February 19 to 85. Human Rights Watch calculates the total dead in four days of protests at 173.

Ruthless Brutality

Human Rights Watch calls on the African Union, the European Union, France, Italy, the United Kingdom, the United States, and other governments with ties to Libya to:

- Publicly demand an end to unlawful use of force against peaceful protesters;

- Announce that those responsible for serious violations of international human rights law must be held individually accountable and will be subjected to appropriate measures;

- Impose an embargo on all exports of arms and security equipment to Libya; and

- Tell Libya to restore access to the Internet.

The Libyan government cut access to the Internet on February 19 and had not restored service on February 20. Craig Labovitz, chief scientist at Arbor Networks, an international network security provider, confirmed that Internet traffic in Libya dropped to zero on February 19 at 2:00 a.m. in Libya.

A lawyer told Human Rights Watch that early on February 19, security officers had arrested Abdul Hafiz Ghogha, one of the most prominent lawyers in Benghazi who represented the families of those killed in 1996 in Abu Salim prison, bringing the total number of activists, lawyers and former political prisoners arrested since the demonstrations began to at least 17.

"In 1996, Libyan authorities killed 1,200 prisoners on one day in Abu Salim and they still haven't acknowledged doing anything wrong that day," said Whitson. "Today the Libyan government has shown the world that it is still using ruthless brutality against its population."

Periodical and Internet Sources Bibliography

The following articles have been selected to supplement the diverse views presented in this chapter.

Kola Afolabi	"Libyan War: Imperialism Pure and Simple," *Black Star News*, March 25, 2011. www.black starnews.com.
BBC News	"Libya: Hague Wants NATO to Take Lead 'Quickly,'" March 24, 2011. www.bbc.co.uk.
Patrick J. Buchanan	"It's Their War, Not Ours," LewRockwell.com, March 10, 2011. www.lewrockwell.com
Judy Dempsey	"Libya Crisis Reveals Splits on E.U. Goals," *New York Times*, April 18, 2011. www.nytimes .com.
Mimi Hall	"Obama: U.S. Will Yield Lead on Libya Operation Soon," *USA Today*, March 22, 2011. www.usatoday.com.
Jonathan Marcus	"NATO and Libya: What Now?" BBC News, April 15, 2011. www.bbc.co.uk.
Ahmed Moor	"A War of Western Imperialism?" *Al Jazeera English*, March 28, 2011. http://english.al jazeera.net.
Ryan Schuette	"Why America Should Intervene in Libya," *PolicyMic*, March 14, 2011. www.policy mic.com.
Dan Weil	"McCain: US Should Lead Libya Operation," Newsmax.com, April 25, 2011. www.newsmax .com.
George Will	"The Tar of Humanitarian Imperialism," FreedomPolitics.com, April 8, 2011. www .freedompolitics.com.

OPPOSING
VIEWPOINTS®
SERIES

CHAPTER 2

How Have WMDs and Terrorism Affected Libya's International Status?

Chapter Preface

Libya agreed to end its nuclear weapons program in 2003. It took six years to complete the process of ridding Libya of nuclear materials. In November 2009, the final batch of enriched uranium for use in nuclear weapons was ready to be removed from Libya. It was wheeled outside the Tajoura nuclear facility near Tripoli, in preparation for being shipped out of the country on a Russian cargo plane specially equipped to carry nuclear materials.

But then something went wrong. According to Max Fisher in a November 27, 2010, post on the *Atlantic* website, "Libyan officials unexpectedly halted the shipment. Without explanation, they declared that the uranium would not be permitted to leave Libya. They left the seven five-ton casks out in the open and under light guard, vulnerable to theft by the al Qaeda factions that still operate in the region or by any rogue government that learned of their presence."

US officials believed the threat of disaster was very real. In a State Department cable of November 25, 2009, officials stated,

> According to the DOE [Department of Energy] experts, we have one month to resolve the situation before the safety and security concerns become a crisis. . . . If the enriched uranium is not removed from the casks in three months, its rising temperature could cause the casks to crack and release radioactive nuclear material.

The casks stayed out in the open for a full month while Libya attempted to extract diplomatic concessions from the United States. According to Lydia Walker writing in a March 18, 2011, post at the Institute of Peace and Conflict Studies, "In this high stakes game, Libya provoked the fear of nuclear terrorism through purposeful neglect. The longer its uranium remained unsecured, the more concessions from the US it hoped to extract." Libya, through Muammar Gaddafi's son Saif al-Islam, variously demanded cash, military armaments, medical facilities, and improved relations.

Eventually, in the face of pressure from both the United States and Russia, Libya backed down. "The matter was resolved when Secretary [of State Hillary] Clinton sent Qaddafi a personal message assuring him of the United States' regard for him and his country. The Russian plane left Tripoli on December 21, 2009," according to Jeremy Bernstein in a February 23, 2011, blog post at the *New York Review of Books*. The incident was a dangerous reminder of the unpredictability of Gaddafi, and of the difficulties involved in securing nuclear materials.

The remainder of this chapter further examines Libya's nuclear program and its links to terrorism.

"*Abandoning its WMD program actually provided Libya more security than continued pursuit of chemical or nuclear weapons.*"

Libya Gained Diplomatic Benefits by Abandoning WMDs

Eben Kaplan

Eben Kaplan is a research associate at the Council on Foreign Relations. In the following viewpoint, he discusses Libya's past history of supporting terrorism and pursuing weapons of mass destruction (WMDs). He also records Libya's decision to move away from these policies. Kaplan notes that the reasons for Libya's change of policy are still being debated. However, he says, Libya did gain security, economic, and diplomatic benefits when it ceased to pursue terrorism and WMDs.

As you read, consider the following questions:

1. What did Libya do in the early 1970s that caused it to be designated a state sponsor of terrorism, according to Kaplan?

Eben Kaplan, "How Libya Got Off the List," Council on Foreign Relations, October 16, 2007. Copyright © 2007 by the Council on Foreign Relations, Inc. All rights reserved.

2. What did Libya do in August 2003 to show it was renouncing terrorism?

3. To what did Vice President Dick Cheney attribute Libya's decision to abandon its WMD program?

On May 15, [2007], Secretary of State Condoleezza Rice announced that the United States was removing Libya from its list of state sponsors of terrorism and would soon resume normal diplomatic relations with the one-time pariah. Rice said the move was in response to "historic decisions taken by Libya's leadership in 2003 to renounce terrorism and to abandon its weapons of mass destruction (WMD) programs." Yet the resumption of diplomatic ties remains unsettling to some Americans. Though Libya has made a concerted effort to enter the good graces of the international community, leader Muammar el-Qaddafi has amassed a bad human-rights record since he took power in 1969.

Why Was Libya Designated a State Sponsor of Terror?

In the early 1970s, Qaddafi established terrorist training camps on Libyan soil, provided terrorist groups with arms, and offered safe haven to terrorists, say U.S. officials. Among the groups aided by Qaddafi were the Irish Republican Army, Spain's ETA, Italy's Red Brigades, and Palestinian groups such as the Palestine Liberation Organization. Libya was also suspected of attempting to assassinate the leaders of Chad, Egypt, Saudi Arabia, Sudan, Tunisia, and Zaire (now Democratic Republic of the Congo).

A Scottish court, convening in the Netherlands for reasons of neutrality, connected Libyans to the 1988 bombing of Pan Am Flight 103 over Lockerbie, Scotland, that killed 270 people. . . . Qaddafi's regime was also implicated in the 1989 bombing of a French passenger jet over Niger in which 171 people died. In 1986, Libya sponsored the bombing of a Berlin disco popular among U.S. servicemen, killing two U.S. soldiers.

Also of concern was Libya's pursuit of WMD. As early as the mid-1970s Qaddafi expressed interest in gaining nuclear-weapons capability to match that of Israel. Libya has been accused of using chemical weapons against Chadian forces during clashes in 1986 and 1987.

One group that Libya never supported was al Qaeda [the international terrorist group responsible for the September 11, 2001, or 9/11, attacks on the United States]. As Libya expert Lisa Anderson told CFR.org's Bernard Gwertzman, al Qaeda regards Qaddafi as "no better than the Saudi government, no better than any of these other governments that they hate." In fact, Qaddafi issued the first Interpol warrant for Osama bin Laden in 1998 for the killings of two German counterterrorism agents in Tripoli four years earlier.

Any nation the U.S. State Department deems a "sponsor of terrorism" faces a range of economic and trade restrictions from the United States. This includes a ban on imports and exports of arms as well as on dual-use items such as equipment that could be used to manufacture chemical weapons. The designated state is ineligible to receive any economic assistance, and U.S. citizens are forbidden from doing business there without express consent from the Treasury Department. Further, the United States suspends the foreign government's diplomatic immunity so that families of terrorist victims may file suit in U.S. courts.

What Did Libya Do to Warrant Removal from the State Sponsors List?

The process of welcoming Libya "in from the cold" began in the late 1990s. The first significant step came in 1999 when, after prolonged negotiations with UN [United Nations] and UK [United Kingdom] representatives, Libya turned over two of its citizens to be tried in the Hague for their role in the Pan Am 103 bombing. Subsequently, [Bill] Clinton administration officials, led by then assistant secretary of state Martin Indyk, began secret negotiations with Libya. Writing in the *Financial Times* in 2004, Indyk recounts Libya's offers to surrender its WMD programs and cut ties to terrorist groups. The U.S. delegation did not accept the offers at the time because of the unresolved investigation into the Pan Am 103 bombing, Indyk says. Though Libya had turned over two Pan Am suspects, it had not accepted responsibility or compensated the families of the victims.

At the same time, Qaddafi increasingly moved to cut Libya's ties to terrorism. Starting in 1999, Qaddafi expelled the Abu Nidal Organization, closed Libya's terrorist training camps, cut ties to Palestinian militants, and extradited suspected terrorists to Egypt, Yemen, and Jordan. In the 2002 edition of the state sponsors of terrorism list, the State Department said Qaddafi had "repeatedly denounced terrorism."

In August 2003, after protracted negotiations with UN, U.S., and UK representatives, Libya finally agreed to pay some $2.7 million in compensation to the victims of the Pan Am 103 bombing. Days later, Libya delivered a letter to the UN Security Council accepting responsibility for the attack.

On December 19, 2003, Tripoli announced it would give up its WMD programs. Back-channel communications with U.S. and UK intelligence agencies had begun in 2002, and secret negotiations continued until just hours before the announcement, as Judith Miller reported in the *Wall Street Journal*. Furthermore, Libya pledged to allow monitors to verify the destruction of the program.

Despite Libya's renunciation of terrorism, several issues give cause for concern. In November 2003, Saudi officials uncovered a plot to assassinate Crown Prince (now King) Abdullah. Human rights monitors continue to rate Libya's record as poor. Though Qaddafi has softened somewhat since the first

Disarming Libya

On December 19, 2003, Libya announced it would dismantle its weapons of mass destruction (WMD) programs and open the country to immediate and comprehensive verification inspections. According to the [George W.] Bush administration, Libya pledged to:

- Eliminate all elements of its chemical and nuclear weapons programs;

- Declare all nuclear activities to the International Atomic Energy Agency (IAEA);

- Eliminate ballistic missiles beyond a 300-kilometer (km) range with a payload of 500 kilograms (kg);

- Accept international inspections to ensure Libya's complete adherence to the Nuclear Non-Proliferation Treaty (NPT), and sign the Additional Protocol;

- Eliminate all chemical weapons stocks and munitions and accede to the Chemical Weapons Convention (CWC); and

- Allow immediate inspections and monitoring to verify all of these actions.

Since December 2003, Libya has also agreed to abide by the Missile Technology Control Regime (MTCR) guidelines, and signed the Comprehensive [Nuclear-]Test-Ban Treaty.

Sharon A. Squassoni and Andrew Feickert,
"Disarming Libya: Weapons of Mass Destruction,"
CRS Report for Congress, *April 22, 2004.*
http://fpc.state.gov.

two decades of his rule—marked by televised hangings and book burnings—those who criticize the national leadership are still jailed. It remains a serious crime to discuss national policy with a foreigner, though prosecutions for such actions have declined. The fate of five Bulgarian nurses charged with deliberately infecting some four hundred children with HIV drew international censure until their eight-year imprisonment ended in July 2007.

Despite its leadership's insistence to the contrary, Libya is far from being a democracy. Qaddafi's son and likely successor, Saif, has denied political aspiration, saying hereditary succession would be undemocratic. But as A.M. Zlitni, Libya's chief economic planner, told the *New Yorker*'s Andrew Solomon, "'Democracy' here [in Libya] is a word that means the leadership considers, discusses, and sometimes accepts other people's ideas." Though that may be the case now, experts say Libya could liberalize in the coming decade, and the resumption of U.S. ties could serve to accelerate that process.

Just as Libya's concessions came in stages, so too did the incentives it received. In February 2004, U.S. officials reopened a diplomatic mission in Tripoli and lifted the travel ban preventing Americans from visiting Libya. Two months later, the diplomatic mission was upgraded to a liaison office. Just over a year later came the announcement that the United States would lift its sanctions and restore full diplomatic relations with Libya.

In October 2007 Libya was voted onto the UN Security Council as a nonpermanent member. Though Washington did not endorse Libya's candidacy, it did not block it either, as it had with previous attempts by Libya to join the Security Council in 1995 and 2000.

Why Did Libya Agree to Make So Many Concessions?

While experts continue to debate Qaddafi's true motivation for abandoning his WMD, security concerns were certainly a factor: abandoning its WMD program actually provided Libya more security than continued pursuit of chemical or nuclear weapons. Another motive was economic. Bruce Jentleson, a Duke University professor and former foreign policy advisor to presidential candidate Al Gore, says Libyan leaders are "gaining economic benefits to deliver to their people," and "a greater chance at domestic stability."

This is the subject of much debate in the foreign policy community. Some suggest Qaddafi feared the [George W.] Bush administration would invade Libya under the preemption doctrine pursued after 9/11. In the 2004 vice presidential debate, U.S. Vice President Dick Cheney said a by-product of U.S. military action in Iraq and Afghanistan "is that five days after we captured Saddam Hussein, Muammar Qaddafi in Libya came forward and announced that he was going to surrender all of his nuclear materials." Others see this more as coincidence than cause and effect. Martin Indyk, for instance, points to Libya's willingness to abandon its WMD in 1999 as evidence that social and economic factors were at the root of Qaddafi's decision. "The economic benefits of being a part of globalization were increasing," says Jentleson. Indeed, pro-Western elements have sprung up among the upper echelon of Libya's leadership. Saif Qaddafi, who is known to have influence among his father's inner circle, has gently urged reform while expressing a desire to lure foreign investment and revitalize the Libyan economy.

"The backdrop of force was a factor, but not nearly the factor Bush and Cheney have portrayed it to be," Jentleson says. "The real story was the diplomacy." Another factor was intelligence. In the first installment of her *Wall Street Journal* article, Judith Miller reports Qaddafi's decision to abandon his WMD was reinforced after U.S. officials gave Libya a compact disc containing recorded conversations between the chief of the Libyan nuclear program and representatives of the Khan network.

"*The U.S. and the international community have demonstrated that WMD is a good insurance policy against interference and attack.*"

Libya Left Itself Open to Invasion by Abandoning WMDs

Paula A. DeSutter

Paula A. DeSutter was US assistant secretary of state for verification, compliance, and implementation from 2002 to 2009. In the following viewpoint, she argues that the United States and Western powers have acted militarily against Libya because Libya renounced weapons of mass destruction (WMDs). She notes that countries with WMD programs, such as North Korea and Iran, terrorize their own citizens with no reprisals. She worries that because of Libya's fate, other nations will decide that they must have WMDs to protect themselves from Western interference.

Paula A. DeSutter, "Libya, WMDs, and Musa Kusa," *National Review Online*, April 4, 2011. http://www.nationalreview.com. Copyright © 2011 by National Review, Inc., 215 Lexington Avenue, New York, NY 10016. All rights reserved.

As you read, consider the following questions:

1. What does DeSutter say impeded Syria's nuclear weapons program?

2. Why does DeSutter believe Musa Kusa was forced to defect from Libya?

3. Why did the foreign service officer that DeSutter quotes say that the United States could treat Libya any way it wanted?

If human rights abuses were the primary determinant of U.S. interventions, then certainly the abuse of the Iranian, Syrian, and North Korean people would qualify at least as easily as the abuse of the Libyan people. [Muammar] Qaddafi [of Libya] is a crazy dictator, but is he really worse than Mahmoud Ahmadinejad [of Iran], Kim Jong-il [of North Korea], or Bashar al-Assad [of Syria]? Libya's killing of peaceful protestors is terrible, but is it more terrible than the torture, murder, and rape perpetrated by the governments of Iran, North Korea, and Syria on their unhappy citizens?

WMDs Are the Difference

Unfortunately, the difference is that while Libya gave up its WMD [weapon of mass destruction] programs, Iran, North Korea, and Syria have kept theirs. Iran and North Korea have aggressive nuclear-weapons programs, and Syria's was impeded only thanks to Israel's attack on their North Korean–built nuclear-reprocessing facility. All three are suspected of having both chemical- and biological-weapons programs, and each is pursuing ballistic missile capabilities of increasing range.

The [Barack] Obama administration has advocated dialogue rather than action in response to these countries' pursuit of WMD programs, and the weakest of responses to their human rights violations. For example, at a June 23, 2009, press conference, President Obama responded to Iran's attacks on peaceful protestors: "The United States and the international community have been appalled and outraged by the threats, the beatings, and imprisonments of the last few days. I strongly condemn these unjust actions, and I join with the American people in mourning each and every innocent life that is lost." He added, however, that "the United States respects the sovereignty of the Islamic Republic of Iran, and is not interfering with Iran's affairs."

Over a year later, on Sept. 23, 2010, speaking to the U.N. [United Nations] General Assembly, President Obama addressed Iran in the context of a world without nuclear weapons: "The United States and the international community seek a resolution to our differences with Iran, and the door remains open to diplomacy should Iran choose to walk through it." Almost two years later, the toughest action the Obama administration has taken is an executive order authorizing the imposition of financial sanctions and visa ineligibilities on eight Iranian government officials who have been tied to the serious human rights abuses surrounding Iran's 2009 presidential election.

Musa Kusa's Defection

The defection of Libya's foreign minister, Musa Kusa [also spelled Moussa Koussa], has been hailed as evidence that the military intervention is having a positive impact. But it is better explained by the role he played in the elimination of Libya's WMD programs.

Musa Kusa has an odd and disturbing background. Kusa went to college in the U.S., where he reportedly became a big fan of Michigan State football. Later he headed the Libyan intelligence services; reportedly, he bears culpability for Pan Am 103 [a plane blown up by Libyan-sponsored terrorists in 1988, killing 270 people] and a domestic reign of terror. He was also, however, the chief negotiator with the U.S. and the U.K. on the possible elimination of Libya's nuclear, chemical, biological, and missile programs.

On Dec. 19, 2003, President [George W.] Bush announced that Qaddafi had "publicly confirmed his commitment to disclose and dismantle all weapons of mass destruction programs in his country.... As the Libyan government takes these essential steps and demonstrates its seriousness, its good faith will be returned." By the end of December 2003, the U.S. and U.K. had agreed on an implementation-and-verification plan, to which the Libyan government agreed in early January 2004. Libya acceded to the Chemical Weapons Convention (CWC) in February 2004, and, in the presence of U.S., U.K., and CWC observers, had destroyed over 3,000 unfilled chemical munitions.

By early March 2004, the U.S. had achieved the most verifiable form of elimination—removal to the U.S.—of over 1,000 metric tons of dangerous nuclear and missile equipment and material. The U.S. also visited chemical facilities that had been converted or eliminated consistent with CWC requirements, as well as facilities that had been part of Libya's biological-weapons program. Libya has been in the process of eliminating its remaining chemical precursors and agents with CWC verification. Libya also agreed not to acquire MTCR [Missile Technology Control Regime]-class missiles and to cease all trade with North Korea and Iran. It began cooperating with the U.S. on counterterrorism.

Musa Kusa, then still the head of Libya's intelligence services, was the individual within the regime who ensured that the elimination was implemented. At the time, I was the head of the State Department's efforts to eliminate WMD in Libya. When the U.S. encountered roadblocks, an approach to Musa Kusa got the effort back on track. On the other hand, when a U.S. news crew went to Libya to try to cover the U.S. role in the elimination of the WMD programs and the lead reporter called me in Washington because they couldn't track down the

American team, I told her to tell her Libyan escorts to call Musa Kusa, since he would be the only one who could give approval for any such access. She repeated my directions to her escorts, then, after a pause, said: "Oooh, they DO NOT want to contact him!" I met Musa Kusa only once, in a U.S./ U.K./Libyan meeting in London. Something about his eyes made the hair on the back of my neck stand up.

The powerful position Musa Kusa had in Libya would suggest that he would be among the last defectors from Qaddafi's regime. I strongly suspect, however, that Kusa's life was at risk at Qaddafi's hand for his role in the elimination of Libya's WMD programs.

The Lesson Learned

While it is hard to complain about getting rid of Qaddafi, the good of Obama and the international community's taking military action is, for me, tainted—because it follows a lack of meaningful response to equally or significantly more brutal abuses by states that possess weapons of mass destruction.

What lesson will be learned in states considering pursuing or retaining WMD programs? If you have no WMD and cooperate with the U.S. on terrorism, but kill protestors, the U.S. and U.N. might enforce tough resolutions, announce that the leader "has to go," and initiate military action. But if you keep or pursue nuclear, biological, chemical, and missile programs, you have little or nothing to fear from the U.S. and the international community—even if you also aggressively support terrorists who kill Americans and others, and arrest, torture, rape, and kill protestors. The U.S. and the international community have demonstrated that WMD is a good insurance policy against interference and attack.

I recall an unpleasant meeting I had early in the second Bush term with a senior foreign-service officer at the State Department. My goal was to explain why we verifiers were interested in moving forward on the positive/carrot parts of the relationship with Libya following the elimination of their WMD programs. We wanted more countries to make the strategic decision not to pursue WMD and to eliminate those programs they were pursuing. I believed it was important to demonstrate that Qaddafi was right when he said that WMD programs make a country less secure.

The senior foreign-service officer disagreed, saying: "Libya is just a weak, unarmed country, and we can treat them any way we want." Apparently he was right.

| "If it hadn't been for those 'armchair warriors' and their 'dumb war' in Iraq, Libya might well be a nuclear weapons power today."

Libya Abandoned WMDs Because of the War in Iraq

Clifton Chadwick

Clifton Chadwick is a blogger. In the following viewpoint, he argues that President Barack Obama was wrong to oppose the war in Iraq. Chadwick says that it was the Iraq war that caused Muammar Gaddafi, Libya's leader, to abandon weapons of mass destruction (WMDs). Chadwick says that if Gaddafi had not been scared into abandoning WMDs in 2003, he would have used chemical and atomic weapons against protestors and rebels in 2011. Chadwick concludes that the war in Iraq was a worthwhile war because it discouraged WMDs and saved many lives.

As you read, consider the following questions:

1. What did Barack Obama call the plan to liberate Iraq?

2. Who is Robert G. Joseph, according to Chadwick?

3. What does Chadwick say Gaddafi told congressional delegations in January and March 2004?

For years, Barack Obama called Iraq "a dumb war." But considering how that conflict undeniably scared Libya's Moammar Gadhafi into ending his WMD [weapon of mass destruction] program, the 2003 invasion has never looked smarter.

Not a Dumb War

"I don't oppose all wars," future President Barack Obama told Chicagoans Against War in Iraq during a 2002 rally. "What I am opposed to is a dumb war . . . a rash war . . . the cynical attempt by . . . armchair, weekend warriors in this ([George W.] Bush) administration to shove their own ideological agendas down our throats, irrespective of the costs in lives lost and in hardships borne."

Obama called the plan to liberate Iraq an "attempt by political hacks like [Republican strategist] Karl Rove to distract us." And he warned that it "will only fan the flames of the Middle East, and encourage the worst, rather than best, impulses of the Arab world, and strengthen the recruitment arm of al Qaeda [the terrorist group responsible for the September 11, 2001, attacks on the United States]."

Goading the then commander in chief, Obama said: "You want a fight, President Bush? Let's fight to make sure that the U.N. [United Nations] (nuclear) inspectors can do their work . . . let's fight to make sure our so-called allies in the Middle East, the Saudis and the Egyptians, stop oppressing their own people."

(This was Obama at his most stupid!!)

Today [in 2011], after two years of President Obama, our "so-called allies" like Egypt are destabilized, or threatened, and in danger of becoming enemies—nothing "so-called" about it.

Turns out that if it hadn't been for those "armchair warriors" and their "dumb war" in Iraq, Libya might well be a nuclear weapons power today. All the U.N. inspectors in the world wouldn't be able to stop Gadhafi from using atomic and chemical weapons to slaughter tens or even hundreds of thousands of his own people to keep himself in power, instead of just conventional weapons to kill a fraction of that number.

Robert G. Joseph, senior scholar at the National Institute for Public Policy in Fairfax, Va., led the nuclear weapons negotiations with Libya nearly a decade ago as undersecretary of state for arms control and special envoy for nuclear nonproliferation during the Bush administration. Joseph recounts what may be the most successful nonproliferation success of modern times in his book *Countering WMD: The Libyan Experience.*

Afraid of What Happened in Iraq

"Multiple motivations were in play as the Libyan leadership worked through the decision to abandon WMD and longer-range missile programs," Joseph writes. The motivations included ending U.S. sanctions.

"There is no evidence to suggest, however, that the goal of ending sanctions would have been sufficient to induce Libya to acknowledge, remove and destroy its WMD programs," according to Joseph. "All evidence suggests that other motives were essential to this outcome."

Joseph stresses that "the timing of the Libyan approach to the United States and United Kingdom, coming as hundreds of thousands of coalition forces were being deployed to the region to enforce U.N. Security Council resolutions on Iraqi WMD, was more than coincidental."

Gadhafi, in fact, told visiting U.S. congressional delegations in January and March 2004 that "he did not want to be a Saddam Hussein and he did not want his people to be subjected to the military efforts that were being put forth in Iraq."

Italian Prime Minister Silvio Berlusconi, in a September 2003 interview, said Gadhafi told him: "I will do whatever the United States wants, because I saw what happened in Iraq, and I was afraid."

As Joseph points out: "Words—that those who seek such weapons will put their security at risk—were being backed by action. In Libya, which had long possessed chemical weapons and had embarked on a large-scale effort to be able to enrich uranium for nuclear weapons, the message was clearly received . . . after Iraq, it would be the next target for U.S. military action."

Had that then unknown, anti-war Illinois state senator [that is, Obama] been listened to in 2002, he would today be a president facing possible nuclear war in the Middle East.

> "It was force and diplomacy, not force
> or diplomacy that turned Gadhafi
> around."

Libya Abandoned WMDs Because of Intelligence, Diplomacy, and Force

Judith Miller

Judith Miller is a writer and journalist. In the following view-point, she argues that Libya's decision to give up weapons of mass destruction (WMDs) was the result of a number of factors. After the September 11, 2001, terrorist attacks on the United States and the subsequent invasion of Iraq, she says, Libyan leader Muammar Gaddafi was afraid of American invasion and hoped that giving up WMDs would normalize relations. Gaddafi was further pushed to abandon WMDs by American intelligence efforts, which were able to show decisively that he was pursuing nuclear weapons. Finally, sanctions and other factors led Gaddafi to believe he would be more secure without WMDs than with them.

As you read, consider the following questions:

1. According to Miller, how much did Gaddafi spend on developing WMDs?

2. At what point does Miller say Gaddafi's enthusiasm for giving up WMDs seemed to wane?

3. By when could Libya have developed nuclear weapons, according to Miller?

As the [George W.] Bush administration struggles to stop Iran and North Korea from acquiring nuclear weapons, it might recall how Libya was persuaded to renounce terrorism and its own weapons of mass destruction programs, including a sophisticated nuclear program purchased almost entirely from the supplier network run by Abdul Qadeer [A.Q.] Khan, the "father" of Pakistan's bomb.

When Libya dramatically declared on Dec. 19, 2003, that it was abandoning its rogue ways, President Bush and other senior officials praised Libya and Moammar al-Gadhafi, the surviving dean of Arab revolutionary leaders, as a model that other rogue states might follow. In fact, the still largely secret talks that helped prompt Libya's decision, and the joint American-British dismantlement of its weapons programs in the first four months of 2004, remain the administration's sole undeniable—if largely unheralded—intelligence and nonproliferation success. And a key figure in that effort, Stephen Kappes, is now slated to be the next deputy director of the demoralized Central Intelligence Agency.

Sanctions and Diplomacy

The post-renunciation diplomacy, however, has not been all smooth. Libyan officials expected that after such a radical change, Washington would generously reward Libya—despite Col. Gadhafi's past terrorist sins and his continuing repression at home. But although the sanctions that helped cripple its

WMD [weapon of mass destruction] programs and oil-dependent economy were lifted, and a small U.S. liaison office was established in Tripoli, Libya remained on Washington's list of states that sponsor terrorism, and full diplomatic relations were not restored, until this week [in May 2006]. While Libya has clearly dawdled, some critics of the Bush administration now argue that Washington's temporizing toward Libya has undermined its nonproliferation victory and has reinforced rogue-state conviction that disarmament will not get one far with Washington. Moreover, the administration quietly continues to attribute Col. Gadhafi's WMD decision to the U.S. invasion of Iraq [in 2003], a claim that has embarrassed Col. Gadhafi among Libyans and his Arab neighbors. Today, the strongman, or Brother Leader as he prefers to be called, is frustrated, and the leadership coterie is restive.

"Giving up WMD alone should have been enough to warrant normalization of relations with the U.S.," Abdellahi El Obeidi, one of Col. Gadhafi's inner circle who now heads the Foreign Ministry's European division, told me during a three-week visit to Libya in March. "We are not where we should be—not at all."

How and why did Col. Gadhafi, the despotic, still dangerously capricious leader, decide to abandon a lifetime of revolution and terrorism and abandon the WMD programs he had pursued since seizing power in a coup in 1969? What role did American intelligence play in that decision? And how much change can Col. Gadhafi tolerate and still retain power?

Col. Gadhafi's hip, 34-year-old son, Saif al-Islam, told me in Vienna—where he earned an M.B.A. and lives when he's not carrying out tasks for his father, or studying for a doctorate in political philosophy at the London School of Economics [and Political Science]—that his father changed course because he *had to*. "Overnight we found ourselves in a different world," said Saif, referring to the Sept. 11 [2001] attacks [on the United States]. "So Libya had to redesign its policies to cope with these new realities."

But a review of confidential government records and interviews with current and former officials in London, Tripoli, Vienna and Washington suggest that other factors were involved. Prominent among them is a heretofore undisclosed intelligence coup—the administration's decision in late 2003 to give Libyan officials a compact disc containing intercepts of a conversation about Libya's nuclear weapons program between Libya's nuclear chief and A.Q. Khan—that reinforced Col. Gadhafi's decision to reverse course on WMD.

While analysts continue to debate his motivation, evidence suggests that a mix of intelligence, diplomacy and the use of force in Iraq helped persuade him that the weapons he had pursued since he came to power, and on which he had secretly spent $300 million ($100 million on nuclear equipment and material alone), made him *more*, not less, vulnerable. "The administration overstates Iraq, but its critics go too far in saying that force played no role," says Bruce W. Jentleson, a foreign-policy adviser to Al Gore in the 2000 presidential campaign and professor at Duke University, who has written the most detailed study of why Col. Gadhafi abandoned WMD: "It was force *and* diplomacy, not force *or* diplomacy that turned Gadhafi around . . . a combination of steel and a willingness to deal."

A Canny Survivor

Clearly, Col. Gadhafi's decision, which Libyans say predated the Iraqi invasion, was part of a broader shift prompted by the miserable failure of his socialist experiment at home, the collapse of the Soviet Union abroad, and his growing conviction that the sanctions which prevented him from expanding oil production—and which isolated him—were jeopardizing his rule.

A canny survivor, Col. Gadhafi first signaled a willingness to negotiate in the early 1990s, soon after the Soviet collapse, officials say. But Washington had little interest in dealing with him then, given his monstrous record on terrorism. Subsequent feelers to the [Bill] Clinton administration went nowhere because they preceded a financial settlement with the families of victims of the [1988] bombing of Pan Am 103 over Lockerbie [a town in Scotland], in which 259 passengers and crew, most of them Americans, had died. Ultimately, Col. Gadhafi agreed to pay $2.7 billion to the Lockerbie families—$10 million per victim—and millions more to compensate families of earlier victims of terrorist attacks. He also accepted Libyan responsibility for terrorist acts committed by two of his intelligence officers while continuing to deny his own obvious complicity in the crime. By then, the Clinton administration was out of office.

Even before 9/11 [September 11, 2001, terrorist attacks on the United States], the Bush administration was focused on unconventional "new threats" to the U.S., particularly WMD in the hands of rogue states and terrorist groups. In his first speech on national security policy, in May 2001, Mr. Bush said he might use force to limit the spread of WMD to those who "seek to destroy us." Deterrence, he said, "is no longer enough."

Col. Gadhafi was alarmed by the new U.S. agenda, and Libyans say that the 9/11 attacks were a turning point for the Brother Leader, who was among the first to condemn them. Through intelligence channels, he sent the administration a list of suspects. He also called Hosni Mubarak [the president of Egypt] in a panic, convinced that Mr. Bush would attack Libya once the Taliban had been crushed in Afghanistan, according to a cable from the U.S. Embassy in Cairo reported last month by *Time*. Meanwhile, Washington increased its rhetorical pressure. Though Libya was not included in Mr. Bush's "axis of evil," then Undersecretary of State John Bolton called Libya a "rogue state" determined to acquire WMD.

In August and the fall of 2002, the British sent emissaries to discuss Libya's unconventional weapons with Col. Gadhafi. At the same time, Saif al-Islam was trying to develop an intelligence back channel to convince the U.S. and Britain that his father wanted a WMD deal. Officials said that Saif initially relied heavily on emissaries, including Mohammed Rashid, a Palestinian who had managed much of [Palestinian leader] Yasser Arafat's money. Though officials recalled that the CIA seemed strangely uninterested in what the Libyan leader's son had to say, MI5, Britain's spy agency, reportedly assured Mr. Rashid that [British Prime Minister] Tony Blair would raise Libya with Mr. Bush when the two men met at Camp David [the country retreat of the U.S. President] in September 2002.

Although the Camp David talks focused mainly on the impending Iraq war, Mr. Bush reportedly accepted Mr. Blair's proposal that they explore Col. Gadhafi's avowed interest in discussing WMD in exchange for lifting sanctions. In October 2002, Mr. Blair wrote a letter to Col. Gadhafi proposing such a dialogue; a few weeks later, Col. Gadhafi replied affirmatively: "I will instruct my people to be in touch with your people," a diplomat quoted his letter as saying. Col. Gadhafi, who Saif says avidly surfs the Net for news, had by now become even more anxious about press reports of Iraqi-Libyan nuclear cooperation. Stories sourced to senior Israeli officials accused Iraq of having sent nuclear physicists to Libya to work on a joint weapons program.

As U.S. and British troops began flooding into Kuwait, Col. Gadhafi grew agitated, diplomats said. Italian press accounts quote then Prime Minister Silvio Berlusconi as saying that Col. Gadhafi had called him to say he feared he would be America's next target. "Tell them I will do whatever they want," said one diplomat, recounting the call. In early March 2003 just days before the start of the Iraq war, Saif and Musa Kusa [also spelled Moussa Koussa], a top Libyan intelligence official, contacted the British to say that Col. Gadhafi wanted to

Libya's Removal from the List

Libyan exile groups expressed dismay yesterday [May 16, 2006] over Libya's removal from the terrorist list. And there will undoubtedly be objections from Congress and elsewhere. But for all the possible questions, Libya stands as one of the few countries to have voluntarily abandoned its WMD [weapon of mass destruction] programs, and out of options for countering Iran's stonewalling, the White House belatedly opted to do more to make Libya a true model for the region. Human rights abuses are more likely to be remedied in a full bilateral relationship.

Judith Miller, "Gadhafi's Leap of Faith,"
Wall Street Journal, *May 17, 2006.*

"clear the air" about WMD programs in exchange for assurances that the U.S. would not try to topple his regime, according to several accounts.

Stalled Talks

In Vienna, Saif told me that the decision to abandon WMD "was my own initiative," an astonishing assertion that no diplomat believes. "The purpose of WMD is to enhance a nation's security. But our programs did not do that," he said. Saif said he had sensed early on that even settling the lingering Lockerbie dispute would not be enough to enable Libya to win Western acceptance. "We needed something bold, something big enough to have impact," he said. "Shock therapy! We knew the Americans would not find yellowcake [partially refined uranium used in nuclear weapons] in Iraq—as we warned them—but that there was yellowcake in Libya, and that this card was worth something." While he rejected the administration's argument that his father had been frightened into abandoning

WMD by the invasion of Iraq, the timing of Libya's overture to the British and Americans was affected by the invasion. "I saw WMD as a card in our hands," he said. The invasion of Iraq was "the best time to play that card."

Washington was skeptical. To prevent leaks and sabotage by neoconservatives and other officials opposed to normalizing relations with Tripoli, details of the Libyan overtures and some half-dozen secret meetings that followed the March overture over the next seven months in London, Geneva and even Tripoli were known to only a handful of senior U.S. officials. Yet as American forces became bogged down in Iraq, Col. Gadhafi's enthusiasm for giving up his WMD programs seemed to wane. Libya had yet to acknowledge even that it possessed banned weapons and programs, a senior official told me. And while the Libyans had agreed in principle to let a team of U.S.-U.K. weapons experts visit sites in Libya, no date had been set. "No agreement on a date meant there was essentially no agreement on a visit," the official said. The talks stalled.

The diplomatic lull soon ended, however. Libyans close to the Gadhafi family told me that after Saddam Hussein's sons were killed in a shootout with U.S. soldiers in Mosul in July 2003, Safia, Col. Gadhafi's wife, angrily demanded that he do more to ensure that Saif and her other sons would not share a similar fate. Then, in early October 2003, the U.S., the U.K., Germany and Italy interdicted the *BBC China*, a German ship destined for Libya that the Americans had been tracking for nearly a year. A U.S. intelligence official informed the Libyans that the five 40-foot containers marked "used machine parts" that were off-loaded from the ship contained thousands of centrifuge parts to enrich uranium, manufactured in Malaysia by the A.Q. Khan network. Stunned by the discovery, Libya fast-tracked its long-promised invitation to the British and U.S. experts to tour suspect sites. A 15-person team, headed by Mr. Kappes, then the CIA deputy director of operations, (who declined to be interviewed for this piece) entered Libya on Oct. 19 on a 10-day mission.

While Col. Gadhafi could have claimed, as Iran now does, that the enrichment equipment was for a peaceful energy program, the pretense was shattered in November when U.S. intelligence gave the Libyans a copy of a compact disc that intelligence agencies had intercepted. According to Saif and Libyan officials in Tripoli, the CD contained a recording of a long discussion on Feb. 28, 2002, about Libya's nuclear weapons program, between Ma'atouq Mohamed Ma'atouq, the head of that clandestine effort, and A.Q. Khan. Denial of military intent was no longer an option.

Libya's Nuclear Progress

The inspection team returned in December 2003, with even greater access. They were astonished by what they learned during their visits to weapons sites, labs and dual-use and military facilities. Although Libya claimed that it had no biological or germ-weapons-related facilities, and that its chemical capabilities were less than the CIA had feared, U.S. intelligence had underestimated Libya's nuclear progress.

Libyan scientists revealed that, between 1980 and 1990, they had made about 25 tons of sulfur mustard chemical-weapons agent at the Rabta facility (which the CIA had long ago identified), produced shells for more than 3,300 chemical bombs, and tried to make a small amount of nerve agent. But they had not mastered the art of binary chemical weapons, in which chemicals come together to form a lethal agent only when the bomb explodes. Thanks to sanctions, a U.S. official wrote recently, Libya was unable to acquire an essential precursor chemical.

The nuclear front was more troubling. Not only had Libya developed highly compartmentalized chemical and nuclear programs that were often unknown even to the Libyans who worked at the facilities, they had already imported two types of centrifuges from the Khan network—aluminum P-1s, (for Pakistan-1), and 4,000 of the more advanced P-2s. By 1997, Libya had already gotten 20 preassembled P-1s from Khan and components for another 200. In 2000, it got two P-2 model centrifuges, which used stronger steel, and had ordered 10,000 more. Libya had also imported two tons of uranium hexafluoride to be fed into the centrifuges and enriched as bomb fuel. In fact, it had managed to acquire from the Khan network what it needed to produce a 10-kiloton bomb, or to make the components for one, as well as dozens of blueprints for producing and miniaturizing a warhead, usually the toughest step in producing an atomic weapon.

Many analysts no longer doubted that Libya could have made a bomb, eventually, if the program had not been stopped and it had found a way to supplement its limited technical expertise. Though most of the rotors for the centrifuges were initially missing (many turned up months later on a ship near South Africa) experts said that had the centrifuges been properly assembled in cascades—always dicey in a technologically challenged state—Libya could have produced enough fuel to make as many as 10 nuclear warheads a year. "We definitely would have done it," said Mr. Ma'atouq, head of the program, just before my tour of Tajura, site of Libya's research reactor and its "hot cells" where scientists could separate fuel for a bomb. "Our original goal was to do so between 2006 and 2008, and if the program was accelerated, by 2007, with a year to spare," he said.

Mr. Ma'atouq confirmed Saif's assertion that Libya had decided to renounce the nuclear and other WMD programs, after months of debate within Col. Gadhafi's inner circle. He said that Libyan experts had advised Col. Gadhafi that the programs no longer served Libyan national interests. "We had discussed many options for securing our state," Mr. Ma'atouq recounted. "I'm an engineer, a practical man. And I said: Let's assume we have these weapons. What would we do with them?

Who is the target? Who would we use them against? The U.S.? We had no delivery system. Yes, nuclear weapons are a deterrent, but it's better to have nothing at all than a deterrent without a means of delivery."

Initially, Mr. Ma'atouq said, Libya had tried to seek Russian help in building a complete nuclear-fuel cycle. But although the Soviets in 1981 had sold Libya the reactor at Tajura, Mr. Ma'atouq complained that they kept raising the price of related material. No deal had been made by the time the Soviet Union collapsed, and by 1995, Libya was left with little choice but to try to develop the bomb indigenously. In 1998, he said, it turned to the Khan network to help "speed things up. We wanted to make the supplier a one-stop shop. We used no other suppliers."

The Khan Network

Relying on the Khan network meant he no longer had to worry about the origin of the equipment and material, or haggle with individual suppliers over the price and (often shoddy) quality of goods on the nuclear black market. He said he never knew (nor wanted to know) where Khan was getting most of what he bought for Libya, though international inspectors say it came mainly from Pakistan, Germany and Malaysia. He claimed that he never knew whether the casks filled with uranium hexafluoride for Libya's gas-enrichment program had originated in North Korea, as U.S. intelligence analysts now believe (based on isotope fingerprints of traces found on the containers).

Col. Gadhafi's decision, though "wise," Mr. Ma'atouq said, had been particularly painful. "I had to prepare the scientists and the technical experts who had worked so hard on different aspects of the program" at Libya's seven separate sites. "It wasn't easy," he said. "This was my program. It was like killing my own baby."

During its second trip in December, the team was taken to sites that U.S. intelligence had not previously spotted and was permitted to photograph and take notes on the astonishing blueprints that few weapons designers had ever seen outside declared nuclear states. The drawings were of a relatively old, crude, but workable design that Pakistan got from China in the early 1960s. The blueprint copies that Khan had provided, as a "sweetener," no less, with their Chinese scribbling still in the margins, had been kept in their original wrappings—a plastic bag from a Pakistani tailor's shop—another bonanza for Western intelligence.

> *"In Libya, as a result of the current strife, literally tons of weapons have recently entered into free circulation where there is little or no government control over them."*

The Libyan War May Be a Major Boost for Terrorism

Scott Stewart

Scott Stewart is an analyst and writer for STRATFOR. In the following viewpoint, he writes that in the past Libya served as a major source of weapons for terrorist organizations. Libyan leader Muammar Gaddafi had backed away from disseminating weapons, but the chaos of the civil war may make many arms, explosives, and perhaps even chemical weapons available again on the black market from Libya, Stewart warns. He concludes that, without a stable government, controlling arms dissemination may be even more difficult than it was when Gaddafi was actively supplying terrorists.

As you read, consider the following questions:

1. What does Stewart mean when he says that weapons are durable?

2. Why are terrorists interested in military-grade explosives, according to Stewart?

3. Stewart says that there is concern that Gaddafi may use what type of weapon against insurgents if he gets desperate?

During the 1970s and 1980s, Libya served as the arsenal of terrorism. While this role may have received the most publicity when large shipments of weapons were intercepted that Libya was trying to send to the Provisional Irish Republican Army [an Irish terrorist group], Libyan involvement in arming terrorist groups was far more widespread. Traces conducted on the weapons used in terrorist attacks by groups such as the Abu Nidal Organization [an anti-Israel terrorist organization] frequently showed that the weapons had come from Libya. In fact, there were specific lot numbers of Soviet-manufactured F1 hand grenades that became widely known in the counterterrorism community as signature items tied to Libyan support of terrorist groups. . . .

Freedom for Jihadists

The conflict in Libya could provide jihadists in Libya more room to operate than they have enjoyed for many years. This operational freedom for the jihadists might have an impact not only in Libya but also in the broader region, and one significant way this impact could manifest itself is in the supply of arms. The looting of the arms depots in Libya is reminiscent of the looting in Iraq following the U.S. invasion in 2003. There are also reports that foreign governments are discussing providing arms to the Libyan rebels in the eastern part of the country. While it is far from clear if any of those discussions are serious or whether any potential patron would ever follow through, past operations to arm rebels have had long-lasting repercussions in places like Afghanistan and Central America.

In light of these developments, a tactical discussion of the various classes of weapons contained in Libyan supply depots and how they could be utilized by insurgents and terrorists is in order.

First of all, it is important to realize that weapons are durable and fungible goods that are easily converted to cash. By durable, we mean that while certain types of weapons and weapon components have a limited shelf life—such as battery-coolant units for the FIM-92A Stinger missile—many other weapons remain functional for many decades. It is not unusual to find a militant or a soldier carrying an AK-47 that was manufactured before he was born—and in many cases even before his father was born. Weapons provided to the anti-Soviet fighters in Afghanistan in the 1980s are still being used against coalition troops in Afghanistan and weapons provided by the United States and the Soviet Union to rebels and governments during Central America's civil wars are still making their way into the arsenals of the Mexican drug cartels. Weapons are fungible in the sense that an AK-47-style rifle manufactured in Russia is essentially the same as one manufactured in China or Egypt, and an M16 manufactured in Israel can easily replace an M16 manufactured in the United States.

One good illustration of the durable and fungible nature of weapons is the fact that some of the weapons seized by the North Vietnamese following the withdrawal of U.S. forces from South Vietnam were traded to Cuba in the 1970s and 1980s in exchange for sugar. The Cubans then provided these weapons to Marxist militant groups in Central and South America. These weapons originally shipped to U.S. forces in Vietnam were then used by insurgents in Latin American civil wars and some of them were even used in terrorist attacks in the 1980s in places such as Chile, El Salvador and Guatemala. More recently, some of these Vietnam-era weapons have made their way from South and Central America to Mexico, where they have been used by the drug cartels. Another example are the Lee-Enfield rifles manufactured in the early 1900s that can still be found in arms markets in places like Yemen and Pakistan. These antiques are still being used by militants in many parts of the world, including Afghanistan, where they have proved to be more effective in longer-range engagements typical of the theater than the newer and more common AK-47s.

The arms depots in Libya have been looted by a number of different actors ranging in motivation from anti-Gadhafi freedom fighters to jihadists to outright thieves and thugs. While the weapons are now being used mostly to fight Col. Moammar Gadhafi's remaining forces, they could later be diverted to other uses. Arms, ammunition and explosives looted from Libyan arms depots today will likely be serviceable for decades, and the thriving transnational black arms market will provide a mechanism for groups and individuals to sell looted weapons or those received from foreign governments. The bottom line is that weapons from Libya will be available on the black arms market for many years to come.

Types of Weapons

So far, the media discussion of Libyan weapons has focused on two classes of weapons: Libya's chemical weapons stockpiles and its "man-portable air defense systems," or MANPADS. These are important to consider in evaluating the threats posed by an uncontrolled military arsenal in Libya, but before discussing these weapons it is worthwhile to look at many other types of weapons that could prove useful to insurgents and terrorists.

One category is small arms, which includes rifles, hand grenades and rocket-propelled grenades (RPGs). A large number of weapons in this class have been looted from arms depots in Libya and widely distributed to rebel fighters. As noted above, such weapons tend to be highly durable and can remain functional for decades. From a militant perspective, such weapons are useful not only in irregular warfare operations but also in armed robberies and kidnappings that are conducted to raise funds for the group. From a terrorism perspective, small arms are useful for assassinations and armed assaults.

Yet another category of munitions of interest to militants is military-grade explosives. Militants in many parts of the world have learned to manufacture improvised explosive mixtures, but such compounds are simply not as compact, stable, reliable or potent as military-grade explosives. Because of this, military-grade explosives have an obvious application for terrorist attacks and are highly sought after on the black arms market.

Still another class is heavier, crew-served weapons, such as heavy machine guns, automatic grenade launchers, recoilless rifles and mortars. Such weapons systems are powerful on the battlefield and can be very useful for insurgents if properly employed, although they are difficult to conceal and transport. Crew-served weapons also use heavier ammunition than small arms and in some cases rapidly consume ammunition, so employing them can also present a significant logistical strain. Because of these factors, they are somewhat difficult to use for terrorist applications. Mortars have been heavily used by insurgents in Iraq, and to a lesser extent by [international terrorist group] al Qaeda in the Arabian Peninsula in Yemen, but these groups have not demonstrated the ability to adjust their mortar fire to effectively engage targets.

MANPADS

Perhaps the biggest worry right now in terms of Libya's uncontrolled military arsenal is the looting of MANPADS, which is quite possibly the biggest blow to worldwide MANPADS counterproliferation efforts since Iraq in 2003. Historically, MANPADS have been very appealing to insurgents and terrorists. Libya is estimated to have at least 400 SA-7 Grail (9K32

An Opportunity for Jihadists

The [2011] uprising in Libya might result not only in a change of ruler but also in a change of regime and perhaps even a collapse of the state. In Egypt and Tunisia, strong military regimes were able to ensure stability after the departure of a long-reigning president. By contrast, in Libya, longtime leader Moammar Gadhafi has deliberately kept his military and security forces fractured and weak and thereby dependent on him. Consequently, there may not be an institution to step in and replace Gadhafi should he fall. This means energy-rich Libya could spiral into chaos, the ideal environment for jihadists to flourish.

Scott Stewart, "Jihadist Opportunities in Libya,"
STRATFOR, February 24, 2011. www.stratfor.com.

Strela-2) surface-to-air missiles in its military inventory. With Libya's largest perceived regional air threat coming from Egypt, it is likely that a substantial portion of its MANPADS stocks were positioned in the eastern part of the country when the current civil war started. We have seen open-source photos of Libyan rebels carrying SA-7 missiles (not always with grip stocks), and one photo even depicted a rebel launching an SA-7 at a pro-Gadhafi warplane. While the air strikes by pro-Gadhafi aircraft have been largely ineffective, the attention these attacks have been receiving in the press could lead some countries to supply additional, and perhaps even more advanced, MANPADS to the Libyan rebels.

As noted in STRATFOR's previous coverage of MANPADS, at least 30 civilian aircraft have been brought down and approximately 920 civilians killed by MANPADS attacks since 1973. These attacks brought about the concerted international effort to remove these weapons from the black and gray arms markets. While MANPADS attacks against civilian aircraft have declined in the last decade, sting operations and seizures of illicit arms shipments clearly demonstrate that militant groups continue to work hard to get their hands on the weapons. This means that any MANPADS not used against pro-Gadhafi aircraft in the current conflict will be sought out by militant groups in the region and by arms dealers, who will seek to sell them elsewhere for a profit.

Artillery Ammunition

The next class of military ordnance to consider—and this is where the chemical threat comes in—is artillery ammunition. A recent video of Libyan arms depots shows that most of the small arms and smaller crew-served weapons have been taken and what is left behind are large stockpiles of artillery ammunition. In Iraq and Afghanistan, insurgents have been able to use artillery rockets to attack large targets like military bases or the Green Zone [where US forces were located] in Baghdad. This fire does not amount to much more than harassment, since the insurgents do not have the skill to deliver the accurate, massed fire required to use such weapons in a militarily effective manner.

That said, artillery ammunition is filled with military-grade high explosives, and militants in places like Iraq, Afghanistan and Algeria have been able to remove the explosive filler from artillery shells, artillery rockets and mortar rounds in order to use it in improvised explosive devices (IEDs). Militants in Iraq also became quite proficient in using artillery rounds (sometimes several of them chained together) as the main charges in roadside IEDs and vehicle-borne IEDs. A 152 mm howitzer shell contains approximately 13 pounds of a high explosive such as TNT or composition B. The explosive fillers used in these rounds are very hardy and include stabilizers that give them virtually unlimited shelf life. Untold thousands of neglected artillery projectiles could very well be the most underappreciated threat in the Libyan arms depots.

And one type of artillery ammunition that has been getting quite a bit of press is artillery ammunition capable of delivering chemical agents. Libya has admitted to producing tons of mustard gas, and the Organisation for the Prohibition of Chemical Weapons is currently in the process of overseeing the destruction of Libya's mustard-gas stockpile (a process no doubt disrupted by the current civil war). There is concern that if Gadhafi gets desperate, he could use mustard gas or some other chemical munitions he had not declared. However, while mustard gas can be deadly if used in high concentrations, it is very difficult to use in a militarily effective manner, which requires a heavy concentration of chemical munitions fire. In World War I, fewer than 5 percent of the troops exposed to mustard gas died. As far as terrorist application, as evidenced by the many chemical attacks conducted by [apocalyptic cult] Aum Shinrikyo in Tokyo and the few chemical shells employed in IED attacks against U.S. troops in Iraq, it is also very difficult to effectively employ chemical weapons in a terrorist attack.

Dangerous Proliferation

In Libya, as a result of the current strife, literally tons of weapons have recently entered into free circulation where there is little or no government control over them. If foreign powers decide to arm the Libyan rebels, more large shipments of arms may soon follow. Given the durable and fungible nature of arms, these weapons could have an impact on the region for many years to come, and Libya could once again become the arsenal of terrorism.

In the past, this role was an intentional policy of the Gadhafi regime, and it was possible to direct international policy against the regime to curtail such activity. In the near future there may not be a stable government with control over all of Libya. The weapons that have been looted from Libyan arms depots have been taken by a number of different actors, and the weapons will almost certainly proceed from Libya via a number of divergent channels. Because of this, controlling these arms may pose an even more difficult challenge than the arms intentionally proliferated by the Gadhafi regime.

> *"Compassion will convince [Libya's Colonel] Qadhafi and senior Libyan officials that they need not be accountable to the law."*

It Is Wrong to Release the Lockerbie Bomber

Mohamed Eljahmi

Mohamed Eljahmi is a cofounder, former board member, and communications officer of the American Libyan Freedom Alliance. In the following viewpoint, he argues that Scotland should not release Abdelbaset Ali al-Megrahi, a man convicted of blowing up Pan Am Flight 103 in 1988. Eljahmi says that Libyan leader Muammar Gaddafi has shown no remorse for orchestrating the bombing. Eljahmi says that releasing al-Megrahi will justify Libyan intransigence and terrorism. He concludes that bargaining with Gaddafi will not change Libya, and only democratic reform can ensure that the country acts responsibly.

As you read, consider the following questions:

1. What is the Megarha tribe, according to Eljahmi?

2. What victims of the Lockerbie bombing does Eljahmi list?

3. What does Eljahmi believe may weaken the resolve of Western politicians?

This week, Scottish authorities are expected to decide whether to release Libyan terrorist Abdelbaset Ali al-Megrahi, or to hold him for the remainder of his sentence. Al-Megrahi was convicted for placing a bomb in Pan Am Flight 103, which blew up over Lockerbie, Scotland, on Dec. 21, 1988. He also suffers from prostate cancer, and Libya has requested his release on humanitarian grounds. But the truth is that Colonel Qadhafi doesn't care about Megrahi's well-being. He cares about consolidating his own power and insuring that by dying in Libya, al-Megrahi remains silent about Qadhafi's role in the terrorist attack.

Al-Megrahi is a member of the Megarha tribe, concentrated in western and southern Libya, who consider themselves to be equals with Qadhafi. The Megarhas serve in key posts in State Security, Intelligence and the Revolutionary Committees. For example, Qadhafi's former deputy, Abdul Salam Jalloud is a prominent member and Qadhafi's present deputy and brother-in-law, Abdulla al-Senussi, is also a Megarha.

On June 4, 1980, Jalloud justified the assassination of Libyan dissidents abroad to an Italian newspaper by saying, "Many people who fled abroad took with them goods belonging to the Libyan people. . . . Now they are putting their illicit gains at the disposal of the opposition led by Sadat, world imperialism and Israel." In June 1996, al-Senussi ordered the mass killing of 1,200 political prisoners at the Abu Sleem Prison in Tripoli. He was also tried and convicted in absentia for the 1989 mid-air bombing of the French airliner UTA Flight 772, in which seven Americans died.

Release of Megrahi would be a blow to the rule of law and also dangerous for Americans. Megrahi asks for compassion, but he has shown none for those he murdered. Among the victims was Michael Bernstein, who devoted his life to bringing Nazis to justice; 66 students of which 35 were from Syracuse University; 20-year-old Theodora Eugenia Cohen, the only child of Susan and Dan Cohen, and 16-year-old Melina Kristina Hudson.

Qadhafi has paid compensation but has never expressed remorse. On April 15, 2007, he said, "We have paid off the compensations to the victims' families, but the U.S. oil companies, which wanted to enter our country, had to pay such fees that they brought this money back to Libya. So, what we gave with the right hand was later taken with the left."

Self-flagellation does not bring justice to American or Libyan victims of Qadhafi. Some members of the families of British victims maintain that their Christian faith compels them to call for Megrahi's release on humanitarian grounds. Megrahi has never shown compassion, though. The Obama administration and Congress must exhibit strong resolve and send an uncompromising message to Scottish authorities and the British government that they must respect the rule of law and the verdict of the court. Compassion will convince Qadhafi and senior Libyan officials that they need not be accountable to the law.

Real security in Libya will only be realized by genuine democratic reform. On March 16, 2004, my late brother Fathi Eljahmi described the dire political situation in Libya in an interview with the U.S.-sponsored al-Hurra TV: "The regime created rampant bureaucracy and institutionalized nepotism and assault on individual liberties. It ordered the confiscation of private properties. . . . All is left for him [Qadhafi] to do is hand us prayer carpet and ask us to bow before his picture and worship him," Fathi said.

After six years of engagement with the U.S., the Libyan leader's regime gained international legitimacy, but its behavior at home has not changed. The Revolutionary Committees and State Security remain a terrorizing force within Libyan society, so reform will not be possible without strong and sustained outside pressure. If released, al-Megrahi will be treated like a hero, and the regime will feel emboldened to commit more domestic atrocities with impunity.

Promise of business deals may weaken the resolve of Western politicians. Playing into the hand of the Libyan strongman is shortsighted, bruises U.S. credibility and does not win the hearts and minds of Libyans.

Rather than the organized mafia they live under, Libyans deserve a democratically elected government for the people, by the people and built on the ideals for which Fathi Eljahmi died.

> "In February 2004, the Libyan prime
> minister told the BBC that his country
> was innocent but was forced to pay up
> as a 'price for peace.'"

Libya Was Framed in the Lockerbie Bombing

Linda S. Heard

*Linda S. Heard is a writer on Middle East affairs and a regular
columnist for* Arab News *and* Gulf News. *In the following viewpoint, she argues that Abdelbaset Ali al-Megrahi was convicted
of the Pan Am Flight 103 bombing over Lockerbie, Scotland, on
the basis of circumstantial and unconvincing evidence. Heard
argues that British and American authorities pushed through a
conviction despite the weakness of the case. Heard concludes that
al-Megrahi should be declared innocent, though she notes that
justice in the case may not be done.*

As you read, consider the following questions:

1. Why did Libya agree to pay compensation to victims'
   families, according to Heard?

Linda S. Heard, "Lockerbie Bombing: Libya Was Framed," GlobalResearch.ca, February
24, 2011. Copyright © Gulf News/Al Nisr Publishing LLC 2011. All rights reserved.

2. On what basis did the Scottish Criminal Cases Review Commission rule that there may have been a miscarriage of justice?

3. Why does Oliver Miles say that no court is likely to get to the truth of the Lockerbie bombing?

On December 21 1988, a Pan Am plane mysteriously exploded over Scotland causing the death of 270 people from 21 countries. The tragedy provoked global outrage. In 1991, two Libyans were charged with the bombing.

Price for Peace

In the event, only Abdelbaset Ali al-Megrahi, a Libyan agent, was pronounced guilty by a panel of three judges, who based their decision on largely circumstantial evidence. Al-Megrahi and the Libyan government have protested their innocence all along.

Nevertheless, after suffering punitive UN [United Nations] sanctions which froze overseas Libyan bank accounts and prevented the import of spare parts needed for the country's oil industry, Tripoli reluctantly agreed to pay $2.7 billion to victims' families ($10 million per family), on condition the payout would not be deemed as admission of guilt.

In February 2004, the Libyan prime minister told the BBC that his country was innocent but was forced to pay up as a "price for peace."

Al-Megrahi is currently [2009] serving a life sentence but earlier this year the Scottish Criminal Cases Review Commission ruled there may have been a miscarriage of justice on the basis of lost or destroyed evidence.

Later this month, a Scottish appeals court is due to revisit the case and is expected to overturn al-Megrahi's conviction as unsafe.

The Libyan leader's son Saif al-Islam recently said he is confident al-Megrahi will soon be found innocent and will be allowed to return home.

On Sunday, an *Observer* exposé written by Alex Duval Smith reported "a key piece of material evidence used by prosecutors to implicate Libya in the Lockerbie bombing has emerged as a probable fake" with allegations of "international political intrigue and shoddy investigative work" levelled at "the British government, the FBI and the Scottish police."

The *Observer* story maintains Ulrich Lumpert a Swiss engineer who was "a crucial witness" has now confessed that he lied about the origins of a timer switch.

Recently, Lumpert gave a sworn declaration to a Swiss court, which read "I stole a prototype MST-13 timing device" and "gave it without permission on June 22, 1989 to a person who was officially investigating the Lockerbie affair."

The owner of the company that manufactured the switch—forced into bankruptcy after being sued by Pan Am—says he told police early in the enquiry that the timer switch was not one his company had ever sold to Libya.

Moreover, he insists the timer switch shown to the court had been tampered with since he initially viewed it in Scotland, saying the pieces appeared to have been "carbonised" in the interim. He also says the court was so determined to prove Libya's guilt it brushed aside his evidence.

In 2005, a former Scottish police chief signed a statement alleging the CIA [US Central Intelligence Agency] had planted fragments of a timer circuit board produced at trial, evidence supporting earlier claims by a former CIA agent to the effect his agency "wrote the script" to ensure Libya was incriminated.

There are also allegations that clothing allegedly purchased by the bomber in Malta before it was wrapped around the bomb, was intact when discovered but by the time it reached the court it was in shreds.

The Convicted Lockerbie Bomber's Legal Team Explains the Grounds of His Appeal

The appellant's [that is, the convicted Lockerbie bomber's] challenge was essentially that there was insufficient evidence to entitle the court to convict, and that, having regard both to the evidence and to the reasoning of the trial court, the verdict was one which no reasonable jury could have returned.

The appellant argued first of all that the circumstantial case as a whole was inherently weak. He went on to examine the inferences which had to be drawn by the court on the way to determining the ultimate question of his guilt. He challenged a number of these crucial intermediate inferences on the basis that either they were not properly supported by the evidence, or they were arrived at by a process of defective reasoning. . . .

Overall the case against the appellant was inherently weak. The circumstantial evidence relied upon by the court to convict was made up of various strands which did not fit together sufficiently coherently and were not substantial enough to carry the weight of a guilty verdict.

Abdelbaset Ali Al-Megrahi,
"Summary of Grounds of Appeal 1 & 2," 2009.
www.megrahimystory.net.

Life Sentence

The shopkeeper who sold the item made a statement to the effect al-Megrahi had never been a customer. Instead, he identified an Egyptian-born Palestinian Mohammed Abu Talb—now serving a life sentence in Sweden for a synagogue bombing.

Professor Hans Köchler, appointed by the UN [United Nations] to be an observer at the trial, has termed its outcome "a spectacular miscarriage of justice." Köchler has repeatedly called for an independent enquiry, which, to date, the British government has refused to allow.

Oliver Miles, a former British ambassador to Libya, insists "no court is likely to get to the truth, now that various intelligence agencies have had the opportunity to corrupt the evidence."

Jim Swire, the father of one of the Lockerbie victims, said "Scottish justice obviously played a leading part in one of the most disgraceful miscarriages of justice in history."

Craig Murray, a former British ambassador, who was earlier second-in-command of Britain's Aviation and Maritime Department from 1989 to 1992, writes about a strange incident on his website.

Murray says a colleague told him "in a deeply worried way" about an intelligence report indicating Libya was not involved in the Pan Am bombing. When he asked to see it, his colleague said it was marked for named eyes only, which Murray describes as "extremely unusual." Earlier, a CIA report that had reached a similar conclusion had been conveniently buried.

If al-Megrahi walks, as is likely, Libya will be vindicated and would presumably be able to reclaim monies paid in compensation along with its reputation.

This would also be a highly embarrassing turn of events for Britain and the US not to mention their respective intelligence agencies, and would leave the question of who bombed Pan Am Flight 103 unanswered. In a perfect world, Libya should also receive an apology from its accusers and should be allowed to sue for damages for all that it lost as a result of UN sanctions.

But in a world where political expediency often triumphs, the appeal has no foregone conclusion despite the exposure of dubious "evidence" and suspect "witnesses."

Periodical and Internet Sources Bibliography

The following articles have been selected to supplement the diverse views presented in this chapter.

Spencer Ackerman	"NATO Is All over the Place on Arming Libyan Rebels," *Danger Room* (blog), Wired.com, March 29, 2011. http://www.wired.com/dangerroom.
Steve Coll	"Don't Arm the Rebels," *New Yorker*, March 31, 2011. www.newyorker.com.
Daily Herald	"Kirk: Arm the Libyan Rebels and Fight Gadhafi Decisively," April 1, 2011. http://dailyherald.com.
Economist	"Libya's Disputed Oil: Better for the Rebels," May 19, 2011. www.economist.com.
Fox News	"Libyan Rebels Will Not Accept Cease-Fire if Qaddafi Stays," April 11, 2011. http://foxnewsinsider.com.
Lourdes Garcia-Navarro	"African Union Hopes to Broker Libya Peace Deal," NPR, April 11, 2011. www.npr.org.
Robert Haddick	"This Week at War: Don't Arm the Rebels, Train Them," *Foreign Policy*, April 1, 2011. www.foreignpolicy.com.
Irish Examiner	"Libyan Rebels 'Will Accept UN Ceasefire,'" April 2, 2011. www.irishexaminer.com.
Emily Esfahani Smith	"US Dilemma: Either Arm Jihadist-Infiltrated Libyan Rebels or Let Gadhafi Prevail," *The Blaze*, March 30, 2011. www.theblaze.com.

OPPOSING
VIEWPOINTS®
SERIES

CHAPTER 3

What Issues Impact Libya's Resistance Movement?

Chapter Preface

In February 2011, a rebellion was launched against Muammar Gaddafi of Libya. One of the major problems that faced the rebel movement was funding. While the West provided air support and launched attacks on Gaddafi's forces, it was reluctant to channel money directly to Libyan rebels.

The most high-profile effort to raise funds occurred in April 2011, when the rebels sold a tanker of oil to Qatar, possibly intended for Italy or France. Libyan oil was under an official embargo. However, a spokesman for the European Union's foreign affairs chief declared, "If revenues don't reach the Khada regime, then we have no issue with commercial dealings in Libyan oil and gas," as quoted in an April 5, 2011, article in the *New York Post*.

Some experts hoped that the oil shipment was a sign "that Libya is back open for international oil trading," according to Michelle Wiese Bockmann of *Lloyd's List*, in an April 5, 2011, interview on *Marketplace*. The oil did raise $100 million for the rebels, but it was not followed by other shipments, and the rebels' need for cash became more and more urgent.

Sanctions against Gaddafi hampered the rebels' efforts to obtain needed supplies, according to Dr. Ali Tarhouni, the head of the rebels' finance office. "Our banking system is frozen, our assets are frozen. We have no access to liquidity. . . . This is a dire situation," he was quoted as saying in a May 18, 2011, article by Theo Leggett of BBC News. Tarhouni raised some money by tunneling into a branch of the central bank in Benghazi and removing cash. He also hoped for cash promised by more than twenty donor countries, but the money was very slow in coming. "It's very frustrating," Tarhouni said. "People are dying."

Doug Saunders, writing in a July 13, 2011, article in the *Globe and Mail*, explained that the rebels' problems were exacerbated by the fact that Gaddafi had "deep reserves of fuel and cash" and was "waging economic warfare with the knowledge that the east [where the rebels are] is running short of everything." For example, Gaddafi appeared to be buying up female sheep, "destroying one of the few remaining food supplies."

Eastern Libya, Saunders noted, should be one of the "wealthiest places in the world," with plentiful oil supplies. But Gaddafi forces damaged the pumping facilities, and the rebels were not able to repair them. Libya is unusually dependent on petroleum; without it, there is no fuel for pumping water or irrigating crops. Getting oil wells back online was therefore vital for the rebels. Faced with these logistical difficulties, the rebels' achievement in defeating Gaddafi's forces, and killing Gaddafi himself on October 20, 2011, was even more impressive.

The remainder of this chapter looks at other aspects of the rebellion in Libya.

"A clear US position on the war over Libya's future would be a major morale booster for the opposition."

The United States Should Arm Libyan Rebels

Amir Taheri

Amir Taheri is an Iranian-born activist and author. In the following viewpoint, he argues that the rebel forces fighting against Muammar Gaddafi need weapons and time if they are to defeat the dictator. Taheri says that if Western forces do not supply weapons, the terrorist group al Qaeda may do so, gaining dangerous influence in Libya. Taheri argues that the Barack Obama administration should stop waffling and should join the French and British in providing aid to the rebels and bringing the conflict to an end.

As you read, consider the following questions:

1. What does Maj.-Gen Suleiman Mahmoud say the rebel forces do *not* need?

2. What does Taheri fear may be the result of a prolonged conflict in Libya?

3. What does Taheri say Gaddafi's daughter has done?

Despite the stalemate settling around the strategic city of Brega, Libyan opposition forces plan to open a front in the west of the country to isolate the capital, Tripoli, which Col. Moammar Khadafy still controls.

More Realism

A western front would cut off Khadafy from his tribal stronghold and from the routes by which African mercenaries join his forces. But to open it, the opposition needs arms, materiel and intelligence that it can't easily secure now.

With NATO [North Atlantic Treaty Organization] assuming command of operations in Libya, the opposition hopes for a more realistic approach from the major Western powers.

"We need help and we need time," says Maj.-Gen. Suleiman Mahmoud, who broke with Khadafy and now commands opposition forces in eastern Libya. "We don't need foreign boots on the ground because we have enough fighters. But we need heavy weapons to match those controlled by Khadafy.

"We can beat him in a fair fight. The world should give us a chance to do so."

Meanwhile, the terrorist groups collectively known as Al Qaeda in the Islamic Maghreb [AQIM], operating in 10 states in northern and western Africa, are trying to secure a foothold in Libya by promising to smuggle arms to the rebels.

Islamist armed groups fought Khadafy in the mountainous Jabal Akhdar region for years. In recent days [March 2011], they've come out of hiding and secured a presence in eastern Libya.

In desperation, anti-Khadafy forces might turn to AQIM for weapons to protect them against the colonel's war machine.

Thus, the Western democracies can't ignore the issue of arming the freedom fighters—though the coalition now seems divided on how much to support the anti-Khadafy forces.

France and Britain appear to favor providing some arms to the opposition. British Prime Minister David Cameron has asked his attorney general to supply an opinion on the legality of such a move, while French President Nicolas Sarkozy has hinted that he is prepared to go it alone, if necessary.

A Clear Position Is Needed

The [Barack] Obama administration, however, seems of two minds. It realizes that, without support for the opposition, Libya may be heading for a prolonged war and morph into a failed state—thus becoming a haven for terrorism on the Mediterranean. Yet some in the administration worry that involvement in a war in an Arab country might undermine President Obama's credentials as "the anti-[George W.] Bush."

Opponents of helping the Libyan freedom fighters cite Russia's statement on Tuesday that arming the rebels would contravene the UN [United Nations] Security Council resolution that allowed the coalition's intervention. But the Russian statement is legally worthless. Russia abstained on the resolution, and thus has no right to interpret it, which it could have done had it voted for or against.

It's also politically worthless, because Moscow won't do anything to counter such a move. It can't ship arms to Khadafy in violation of the UN-imposed ban, and wouldn't be stupid enough to try to physically block the supply of materiel to Libyan opposition forces.

American ambiguity over Libya can only prolong the conflict—which is in no one's interest. A long conflict would only mean more death and devastation and could provoke a refugee crisis that could affect the fragile new regimes in Tunisia and Egypt.

By contrast, a clear US position on the war over Libya's future would be a major morale booster for the opposition. It would also encourage more of Khadafy's shrinking entourage to abandon him—as Foreign Minister Moussa Koussa [also spelled Musa Kusa] just did, arriving in London to demand political asylum. (I reported that Koussa was planning to defect in the March 19 *Post*.)

Koussa is the fifth member of the Khadafy Cabinet to defect—and the most important. A cousin of the colonel, he led the regime's intelligence service for years and negotiated the ending of Libya's nuclear and chemical-weapons programs with [then secretary of state] Condoleezza Rice.

Libyan sources tell me that Koussa's move heralds further defections within the Khadafy clan: Khadafy's daughter Ayesha has already fled to Vienna and may soon appear in public to denounce her father's dictatorship.

> "The introduction of American-made weapons into the hands of the rebels will undoubtedly change the very nature of the current conflict."

Arming Libyan Rebels Would Be Dangerous

Daniel R. DePetris

Daniel R. DePetris is an associate editor of the Journal on Terrorism and Security Analysis. *In the following viewpoint, he argues that the initial United Nations mission in Libya was to protect civilians. He says that providing weapons to the Libyan rebels would be a dangerous extension of the mission and could actually extend the conflict, endangering more civilians. He also says that involving the United States would undermine the idea that the rebellion was led by Libyans and may cause a backlash against the United States. He concludes that the United States and other nations should provide humanitarian aid but not weapons.*

Daniel R. DePetris, "Arming Libyan Rebels Dangerous Proposition," *Washington Note*, April 6, 2011. http://www.thewashingtonnote.com. Copyright © 2011 The Washington Note. All rights reserved.

As you read, consider the following questions:

1. According to DePetris, how have Democrats and Republicans reacted to the Barack Obama administration's actions in Libya?

2. What is mission creep, and how does DePetris say it was exemplified in Vietnam?

3. Why does DePetris say Washington should step up its contacts with Arab and African leaders?

Amid criticism from congressional Republicans that the United States "dithered" in Libya, as well as complaints from his own party, President Barack Obama addressed the nation a week ago Monday [April 2011] in an attempt to address those concerns and put them to rest. And while questions remain as to when the conflict will end and what the United States is ultimately trying to accomplish in Libya, the president put forth a compassionate case for his decision to intervene. Indeed, as Obama stated, tens of thousands of Libyan civilians in the eastern portion of the country could have been susceptible to a systemic wave of violence if the international community did not respond in time.

Making the Case

"We knew that if we waited one more day, Benghazi—a city nearly the size of Charlotte—could suffer a massacre that would have reverberated across the region and stained the conscience of the world," Obama said. "It was not in our national interest to let that happen. I refused to let that happen."

Clearly, the speech was not only a defense of the president's policy, but the first step in a series of efforts by the administration to ensure everyone that matters that the White House is on the same page and knows what it is doing.

A day later, Admiral James Stavridis, the head of US European Command and the man in charge of the Libya operation, testified in front of the Senate Armed Services Committee to tout the White House line. Secretary of Defense [SecDef] Robert Gates and the Director of the Joint Chiefs of Staff [JCS], Admiral Mike Mullen, followed up on those remarks with testimonies of their own on March 31, facing critiques by both parties about the administration's military objectives.

Mr. Gates and Gen. Mullen, in a packed chamber, did a relatively decent job of explaining the administration's narrative in the Libya conflict. Congressional support for the humanitarian mission thus far has been spotty, with Democrats warning against escalation, Republicans lambasting the White House for not doing enough to support the rebels, and both charging the administration with avoiding Congress during the deliberation phase before Tomahawk cruise missiles rained down on Tripoli.

Yet there was one question asked during the Senate and House hearings that Gates and Mullen strayed away from, clearly for the purpose of keeping all of the president's options on the table. Is the United States going to send weapons to the Libyan rebels?

US officials are already debating this question amongst themselves. Perhaps we should not be surprised that SecDef Gates and JCS Chairman Mullen evaded the question. Indeed, there appears to be a general disunity among White House staff, the State Department, and the Pentagon on whether funneling arms to anti-Qaddafi forces is a viable, or smart, alternative.

Mission Creep

Just the fact that US officials are having this discussion exemplifies a classic case of "mission creep," which can be briefly described as the tendency of a military operation to escalate as time goes on. In Afghanistan, the original mission for Washington was to route al Qaeda training camps, drive the Taliban from power, and kill or capture the man responsible for the

The Dangers of Arming Rebels

The story of arming rebels is the story of one of the unrecognized tragedies of our time: small arms proliferation. The abundance of cheap and increasingly deadly weapons fuels regional arms races and escalates the most minor conflicts; armed conflict is much more viable when the tools of violence are easy to come by.... For all the attention paid to nuclear proliferation, small arms impose a far heavier human toll.

Diana Wueger,
"The Global Risk of Arming Libya's Rebels,"
Atlantic, *April 8, 2011.*

September 11 [2001] attacks [on the United States]. Ten years later, the United States military and its allies are stuck in a fight with an adaptive and homegrown enemy, with goals that far exceed the original plan.

Vietnam is perhaps the most obvious case of mission creep. In 1963, the United States followed the specific order of "advising" South Vietnamese troops for their war against the communists in the north. Six years later, 500,000 American soldiers found themselves in the jungles of Vietnam in a misguided notion that the North Vietnamese could be defeated by military power alone.

Fast-forward to 2011, and Washington could very well be traveling down the same rugged path. Despite all the bombing runs and cruise missile attacks from coalition warplanes, the central mission as stated in the UN [United Nations] Security Council resolution is still the protection of Libyan civilians. This is precisely why a no-fly zone is up and running over Benghazi and eastern Libya, and why coalition planes continue to strike Qaddafi's mobile military forces on the ground.

But the introduction of American-made weapons into the hands of the rebels will undoubtedly change the very nature of the current conflict. One of the most captivating stories over the past three months is the notion that the Arab people themselves are taking action against their own corrupt and nepotistic governments, without overt foreign support or another Western-led invasion akin to 2003 Iraq.

Arming the Libyan rebels would drastically undercut that compassionate narrative, once again placing the United States and its Western allies smack in the middle of a conflict that Libyans started, and must finish. Covert support may weaken Qaddafi's power base and shorten the time that he is in power, but it could also prolong the war by adding more firepower to the other side. More suffering by the Libyan people would be a result, which ironically would refute the entire resolution that the Security Council passed before the Libyan intervention began.

If the West wants to help, sending in humanitarian supplies and urging Western and Islamic charities to treat civilians who are struggling is the safest and most humane option. Washington would also be advised to step up their contacts with Arab and African leaders in the hopes of offering Qaddafi and his family a way out. This option would not be the punishment that Qaddafi deserves, but it could cut the duration of the war effort significantly and speed up post-conflict rebuilding.

Otherwise, Washington should stay out of this civil war and redirect resources on issues that really matter for US interests and the continued momentum of the "Arab Spring": smoothing Egypt's transition to a parliamentary system, urging Saudis to withdraw their troops from Bahrain, and calling for reconciliation among Yemen's many factions. All in all, ensuring that Egypt makes a complete break with its authoritarian past will be a greater precedent for democracy advocates in the Arab world than the overthrow of an isolated, and marginal, North African dictator.

> *"[Libyan leader Moamer] Kadhafi and his sons must leave immediately if they want to be safe. . . . Any initiative that does not include the people's demand, the popular demand, essential demand, we cannot possibly recognise."*

The Rebels Can Accept Peace Only if Gaddafi Steps Down

US Africa Online

US Africa Online is a US-based, African-owned online newspaper. In the following viewpoint, the paper reports that Libyan rebels rejected a peace deal with leader Muammar Gaddafi brokered by the African Union. The paper says that the rebels insist that for any peace deal, Gaddafi and his sons must leave the country. The rebels believe that only if Gaddafi leaves can peace and democracy come to Libya. In the meantime, the paper reports, violence continues between the rebels and Gaddafi, with North Atlantic Treaty Organization (NATO) forces also launching attacks on Gaddafi's troops in an effort to protect civilians.

Editor's note: Libyan dictator Muammar Gaddafi was captured and killed by rebel forces near his hometown of Sirte on October 20, 2011.

As you read, consider the following questions:

1. What are the US goals in Libya, according to Secretary of State Hillary Clinton?

2. What groups does Libya say it is willing to accept humanitarian aid from, according to the viewpoint?

3. What does Moussa Koussa fear will happen if civil war breaks out in Libya?

Libyan rebels on Monday [in April 2011] rejected an African Union initiative for a truce accepted by Moamer Kadhafi, and said the only solution was the strongman's ouster, an idea his son called "ridiculous."

Kadhafi Must Depart

The rebel rejection came after NATO [North Atlantic Treaty Organization] chiefs warned that any deal must be "credible and verifiable," and as alliance warplanes were again in action against heavy Kadhafi weaponry pounding Ajdabiya and Misrata.

US Secretary of State Hillary Clinton also stuck to US demands for Kadhafi to step down and leave Libya as part of a peaceful transition, but declined to comment on the proposed African Union deal before being fully briefed.

"We have made it very clear that we want to see a ceasefire, we want to see the Libyan regime forces pull back from the areas they have forcibly entered," she told a news conference in Washington.

"We want to see humanitarian assistance reach the people of Libya. These terms are non-negotiable.

"We believe, too, that there needs to be a transition that reflects the will of the Libyan people and the departure of Kadhafi from power and from Libya."

Kadhafi's son Saif al-Islam admitted that it was time for "new blood" in Libya, but called talk of his father stepping down "ridiculous."

"The Libyan Guide (Kadhafi) does not want to control everything. He is at an advanced age. We would like to bring a new elite of young people onto the scene to lead the country and direct local affairs," he told France's BFM TV.

"We need new blood—that is what we want for the future—but talk of the Guide leaving is truly ridiculous," he added.

In Benghazi, rebel leader Mustafa Abdul Jalil said the African initiative did not go far enough.

"From the first day the demand of our people has been the ouster of Kadhafi and the fall of his regime," he said.

"Kadhafi and his sons must leave immediately if they want to be safe. . . . Any initiative that docs not include the people's demand, the popular demand, essential demand, we cannot possibly recognise."

Violence Continues

NATO said it struck more loyalist targets around Ajdabiya and the besieged port of Misrata on Sunday and Monday, destroying 11 Kadhafi regime tanks and five military vehicles.

The regime warned that any foreign intervention under the pretext of bringing aid into Misrata would be met by "staunch armed resistance," the official JANA news agency quoted the foreign ministry as saying.

"Libya will only accept humanitarian aid from the Red Cross and the Red Crescent," it said, adding that it had informed the UN [United Nations] Security Council, the European Union [EU] and the African Union of its position.

Power Sharing Is Unlikely

[Power sharing between Libyan leader Muammar Gaddafi and rebels] is very unlikely for a number of reasons. First of all, the international coalition has emphatically declared that Gaddafi cannot be part of any government and that he must face justice.... Secondly, the rebels have already rejected a power-sharing agreement that would include *any* Gaddafi. Thirdly, given Gaddafi's track record, there is little reason to trust that he would be sincere in implementing a power-sharing peace agreement.

Mark Kersten,
"Libya, Peace and Justice: Murky Options,"
Justice in Conflict *(blog), April 20, 2011.*
http://justiceinconflict.org.

Diplomats in Brussels [Belgium] said on Friday that the EU was gearing up to deploy military assets for a humanitarian mission to evacuate wounded from Misrata and deliver food, water and medicine to the city.

NATO chief Anders Fogh Rasmussen warned that warplanes will keep pounding Libyan forces as long as civilians are at risk.

"I would also like to stress that the guiding principle for us will be how to implement the UN Security Council resolution fully, that is to protect the civilians against any attack," he said.

Shamsiddin Abdulmolah, a spokesman for the rebels' Transitional National Council, welcomed the African Union efforts, but demanded Kadhafi's overthrow.

"The people must be allowed to go into the streets to express their opinion and the soldiers must return to their barracks," he told AFP [a global news agency].

"If people are free to come out and demonstrate in Tripoli, then that's it. I imagine all of Libya will be liberated within moments."

He also demanded the release of hundreds of people missing since the outbreak of the popular uprising and believed to be held by Kadhafi's forces.

South African President Jacob Zuma said earlier that Tripoli had accepted the African Union plan for a cease-fire.

"We also in this communique are making a call on NATO to cease the bombings to allow and to give a cease-fire a chance," he said.

But White House spokesman Jay Carney told reporters: "Our response to the quote, unquote, cease-fire is what matters here are actions and not words.

"Colonel Kadhafi and his regime know full well what they need to do," he said, adding that Washington was not letting up in implementing the UN Security Council resolution in any way.

"The implementation continues and will continue as long as necessary. We continue to pursue our diplomatic and economic measures to tighten the noose around Kadhafi."

The rebels doubted Kadhafi would adhere to a truce anyway.

"The world has seen these offers of cease-fires before and within 15 minutes (Kadhafi) starts shooting again," Abdulmolah said.

The rebels have said they would negotiate a political transition to democracy with certain senior regime figures, but only on the condition that Kadhafi and his sons leave Libya.

Meanwhile, Libya's former foreign minister Moussa Koussa [also spelled Musa Kusa], who is in Britain after defecting from Moamer Kadhafi's regime, said Monday the restive nation could become a "new Somalia" [an African nation that descended into chaos after years of civil war] if civil war broke out.

"I ask everyone, all the parties to avoid taking Libya into a civil war," the former minister said in a statement issued to the BBC.

"This would lead to so much blood and Libya will be a new Somalia," he said. "We refuse to divide Libya. The unity of Libya is essential to any resolution and settlement for Libya."

"What lies ahead is frightening. For as long as the West props up the rebels and destroys pro-Gaddafi forces and arsenal, the Libyan crisis is nowhere near solution soon."

The Rebels Should Have Accepted a Peace Deal and Negotiations with Gaddafi

Michael J.K. Bokor

Michael J.K. Bokor is assistant professor of English at the Brooklyn Campus of Long Island University. In the following viewpoint, he argues that the conflict in Libya is essentially a political struggle. As such, he says, it requires a political, not a military, solution. He argues that the rebels' decision to reject a peace deal offered by the African Union will lead to a protracted conflict. He says that neither side can win quickly and that the result of ongoing fighting will be a tragedy for Libya.

Editor's note: Libyan dictator Muammar Gaddafi was captured and killed by rebel forces near his hometown of Sirte on October 20, 2011.

As you read, consider the following questions:

1. Who made up the African Union delegation, according to Bokor?

2. What does Bokor say the African Union deal proposed?

3. According to Bokor, why did Gaddafi accept the African Union peace plan?

The tired saying may be right after all: "Show me your friend, and I will tell you your character."

No Peace

Even without weighing the long-term implications of the African Union [AU] delegation's "Road Map for Peace," the Libyan rebels have rejected the offer to end hostilities and use political solution as the compass to show a new direction for their country. I am not in the least surprised at this rejection.

The rebels said they were rejecting the truce because it did not include plans for Col. [Muammar] Gaddafi to step down (according to the BBC news report dated 04/11/11). The AU delegation gave faint hints that such an issue was not completely ruled out of negotiations even though they would not openly confirm or deny it as part of the terms.

The presidents of South Africa, Mauritania, Mali, and Congo-Brazzaville, and the Ugandan foreign minister made up the AU delegation. We are told that the delegation's mission was endorsed by the European Union/NATO [North Atlantic Treaty Organization], suggesting that the Western militaristic establishment has, after all, seen sense in a political solution to the crisis.

The rebels' repudiation of the AU delegation's overtures is not surprising since we know very well that the one and only factor that caused the rebellion was opposition to Gaddafi's continued stay in office. Unlike the economic factors that motivated protesters in Tunisia, Egypt, Algeria, and other parts in the Arab world, the Libyan uprising stemmed from abhorrence for Gaddafi's long rule and fears that he might pass the baton on to his son—creating a dynasty. The Libyan crisis has more political currents than anything else. Thus, any solution that doesn't overtly say that "Gaddafi must go" will be still-born. It won't see the light of day in the camp of the rebels.

Also not to be considered as favourable is the part of the AU delegation's term that calls for the suspension of NATO air strikes. The rebels know very well that without NATO air strikes, they stand no chance of realizing their aspirations against the pro-government forces. Rejecting the overtures on account of this term alone is a matter-of-course.

On its own, though, the AU's peace plan isn't skewed to favor Gaddafi. At least, the terms are clear. The AU deal proposed:

- An immediate cease-fire;

- The unhindered delivery of humanitarian aid;

- Protection of foreign nationals;

- A dialogue between the government and rebels on a political settlement; and

- The suspension of NATO air strikes.

Rather intriguingly, a spokesman for the rebels (Mustafa Abdel Jalil from the rebels' Transitional National Council (TNC)) had this to say at a news conference in Benghazi: "The African Union initiative does not include the departure of Gaddafi and his sons from the Libyan political scene; therefore it is outdated." He added that "the initiative speaks of reforms from within the Libyan system and that is rejected."

These words are not unexpected. The rebels know where their bread is buttered. The US, the UK and Italy have again said the Libyan leader must leave, which is the banner slogan for the rebels. Both NATO and the rebels are singing the same song and will not change this tune just because the AU says

NO FLY ZONE

(AR) THE CLARION CALL. 3/31

so. They know that the AU itself is under the armpit of the West and lacks bite. Its opposition to the military option is ineffectual as far as they are concerned.

Overreaching

The confidence level of the rebels is too high for them to descend from their high horse to accept the AU delegation's proposal. Bolstered by the International Coalition's persistent disabling of the pro-government forces' military capabilities, these rebel forces may feel that a military victory is certainly their gateway to ousting Gaddafi from power. They will not be willing to relent in this bid.

Furthermore, they are looking into the near future to conclude that they will soon have enough military hardware to face up to the pro-government forces. Why should they relent when there is a silver lining on the horizon for them? Having already dispatched the first batch of crude oil for sale through Qatar, they are assured of armaments and consider the sophisticated weapons to be given them by their backers in the West and Qatar as the succor they need to remove Gaddafi from office.

The assurances given by NATO and the persistent calls by high-ranking government officials in the West that the Libyan crisis can be resolved only when Gaddafi "goes," seems to have impelled these rebel forces to fight to the end. They are confident that with NATO's support, they will prevail over the pro-Gaddafi forces.

If the absence in the AU's terms of any direct call for Gaddafi to hand over power and leave Libya is why the rebels have rejected the AU's peace overtures, then, the rebels may be biting off more than they can chew. Or they may just not want to give peace a chance. They may be wary of the AU delegation's motives, as they've already begun accusing it of taking sides and being sympathetic to Gaddafi's cause. Of course, who will blame them? Knowing very well how much influence Gaddafi wields in the AU, the rebels should naturally be cautious in responding to the AU's overtures. But rejecting it outright is impolitic because it immediately shuts the door on any negotiation that is envisaged under the peace plan.

On his part, Gaddafi didn't hesitate at all in accepting the AU's terms, which indicates that he is confident in a political solution, unlike the rebels who think that the military option is better.

Political Problems, Political Solutions

By now, it must be clear that the Libyan political problem cannot be solved by the military option. Political problems must be solved politically, not militarily. At this time that NATO is seriously poised against the pro-Gaddafi forces alone, indications are clear that both sides have reached a stalemate, which the AU's peace overtures can help resolve if accepted by both sides. Considering the ding-dong battles going on (and the shifting fortunes), it is clear that neither side can dislodge the other from territories under its control. Misrata, for instance, is shared between the pro-Gaddafi forces and the rebels. So also is Ajdabiya, which seems to be suffering a similar fate. Running battles are the order of the day.

As the stalemate drags on and NATO continues to destroy Libya's military assets under the guise of incapacitating Gaddafi's forces, the Libyan crisis will continue to attract public interest. The scenario is, however, likely to shift to a higher gear when the rebels receive consignments of weapons equal to what the Libyan government forces use or even more powerful than what they are scared of for now. With such armaments, they may have some confidence to extend their onslaught to territories now in the hands of the Libyan government. More blood will definitely be shed—but NATO and the UN or the West will cry foul only if it is the pro-Gaddafi forces that are alleged to be doing the killing. They don't regard the atrocities committed by the rebels they are supporting as worth their (or anybody's) bother.

I can infer from the hot-headedness of the rebels and their Western backers that they are bent on carrying the fight to Gaddafi in Sirte and Tripoli. Now that the rebels have begun flying MIG fighter aircraft, they may step up their invasion and hope that NATO will do the hatchet job to draw them close to the object of their hatred.

What lies ahead is frightening. For as long as the West props up the rebels and destroys pro-Gaddafi forces and arsenal, the Libyan crisis is nowhere near a solution soon. The problem seems to have been compounded by this intransigence on the part of the rebels. By rejecting the AU's peace initiative outright, the rebels have erected more barriers on the road. It is not yet clear what the AU will do next. If it decides to return to Benghazi, it will have to revise its peace plan and hold prior consultations with Gaddafi to work out the demand for him to leave Libya.

That's where the sticky point emerges because Gaddafi has all along insisted that he will not leave his country on any account just to appease the rebels and their backers in the West. The stage seems to be set for a long drawn-out and complicated military engagement in Libya.

Maybe, as time goes on, public opinion in the West and Africa will shift to suggest more emphasis on the political solution. It must be clear by now that the military option will not solve the Libyan crisis. At best, it will only cause a total destruction of the country, which may be what the West is looking for because rebuilding Libya (in all senses) will be done by business interests in the West!!

On the other hand, if the crisis degenerates into a civil war, it will complicate matters further and prove to the West that they have all along been betting on the wrong horses in Benghazi. The Libyans themselves know the root causes of their crisis and should determine how to resolve it without all these sophisticated weapons being introduced into the equation.

The clock may be ticking slowly but it will definitely reach the point for those now bombarding Libya to the advantage of the rebels to realize that they have all along been chasing a mirage in the Sahara desert.

> "If not with [Libyan leader Muammar]
> Gaddafi himself, then the rebels and
> the international coalition behind them
> will have to negotiate with those who
> remain loyal to him."

Negotiating Gaddafi's Departure Will Be Extremely Difficult

Mark Kersten

Mark Kersten is a doctorate student in the International Relations Department at the London School of Economics and Political Science. In the following viewpoint, he argues that Muammar Gaddafi retains surprising loyalty in Libya. As a result, he says, no decisive victory for either side seems likely, and that means that at some point there must be negotiations with Gaddafi or his supporters. This may mean, Kersten says, that peace may require letting Gaddafi go free. However, Kersten concludes, peace and justice are not always at odds, and it is possible that efforts to bring Gaddafi to justice may aid the peace process.

Editor's note: Libyan dictator Muammar Gaddafi was captured and killed by rebel forces near his hometown of Sirte on October 20, 2011.

As you read, consider the following questions:

1. What does Kersten say is a truism among scholars and practitioners of conflict resolution?

2. As stated by Kersten, why did the rebels reject the African Union peace deal?

3. According to Kersten, what are the bad options that would ensure that Gaddafi was not at the other end of the peace negotiation table with the rebels?

M issing from the coverage of the war in Libya has been any discussion as to what the end goal is. Yes, there has been a lot of talk, although little consensus, about what should happen with [Libyan leader Muammar] Gaddafi. But what about Libya itself? When the coalition partners involved in the mission in Libya ask themselves "where do you see Libya in five years" what is their answer?

What Happens After the War?

What is the international community trying to achieve, and more importantly what is *possible* to achieve? Is the aim to have the current rebels controlling the country? Perhaps a leader, handpicked by the coalition powers, will be chosen to oversee a transition to democracy?

Lost in the midst of the chaotic and equally ambiguous mission in Libya are questions regarding what happens when the bombing ends. The conventional wisdom of conflict resolution suggests that *only* a negotiated settlement between the rebels and the pro-Gaddafi factions can guarantee peace. That may clash with another goal of the mission: justice.

It is an accepted truism amongst scholars and practitioners of conflict resolution that unless there is a clear victor in an armed conflict, a negotiated peace agreement is necessary.

Conflicts that end in negotiated agreements, rather than military victory by one party, tend to include provisions for power-sharing between the conflicting parties. The hope is that power-sharing can reassure previously conflicting parties about key issues concerning the control of and access to economic resources, political power and security. It is argued that power-sharing is particularly necessary where the social fabric of a society has particularly sharp ethnic, religious, regional, or other, tensions.

In a recent paper, *Power-Sharing and Transitional Justice: A Clash of Paradigms?*, Stef Vandeginste and Chandra Lekha Sriram (2011) argue that the paradigms of post-conflict power-sharing and accountability clash. Where conflicts have included mass atrocities, a typical response has been to grant amnesty laws or offer exile to perpetrators as an incentive to continue the process of negotiating peace.

A problem arises when attempting to provide a place for justice in power-sharing agreements. The problem is exacerbated because, as Michael Scharf notes, it is unrealistic to believe that a party would cease hostilities if "they would find themselves or their close associates facing life imprisonment." For some, like Jack Snyder and Leslie Vinjamuri, this reflects the rather uncomfortable reality that, for some, the perpetrators of atrocities may sometimes be "indispensable allies" in the pursuit of peace.

Peace and Justice in Conflict

Let's apply the theory to Libya. The past few weeks have shown that Gaddafi retains a remarkable, perhaps surprising, level of support within Libya. The result, as characterized by the *Economist*, has been constant "see-sawing" in the fighting between pro-Gaddafi forces and the rebels. The divisions within the social fabric of Libya are clearly profound and, according to some, the outbreak of war along tribal lines remains a distinct possibility. While it is difficult to ascertain where it derives from and how strong it is, it does not appear that Gaddafi retains significant levels of loyal support.

All of this may suggest that a negotiated settlement, with power-sharing provisions, between the rebels and pro-Gaddafi forces is the only way to end the conflict. Interestingly, this was recognized in an attempt to broker a truce by the African Union. Gaddafi accepted their plan, which included a "dialogue between the government and rebels on a political settlement." The rebels subsequently rejected it on the basis that "[t]he African Union initiative does not include the departure of Gaddafi and his sons from the Libyan political scene."

If it is increasingly evident that, at the current pace, there will be no decisive victor in Libya. Yet the ambivalence about what should be done with Gaddafi has been replaced by a vehement consensus that "it is impossible to imagine a future for Libya with Qaddafi in power." In their now infamous letter, President [Barack] Obama, President [Nicolas] Sarkozy [of France] and Prime Minister [David] Cameron [of Britain] declared:

> "The International Criminal Court [ICC] is rightly investigating the crimes committed against civilians and the grievous violations of international law. It is unthinkable that someone who has tried to massacre his own people can play a part in their future government. The brave citizens of those towns that have held out against forces that have been mercilessly targeting them would face a fearful vengeance if the world accepted such an arrangement. It would be an unconscionable betrayal."

Meanwhile, there are reports that the US and others are seeking states to offer Gaddafi asylum. Uganda recently declared that it would welcome Gaddafi.

A number of observers have argued that the ICC's investigation of Gaddafi may make the chances of peace less likely. It is an argument based on a lot of assumptions of what conflict resolution entails and what incentives exist in negotiating peace. It is also an unbalanced argument which fails to consider counter-narratives. Doug Saunders, for example, recently argued that justice "stands in the way of" Gaddafi's departure:

> "By applying the pressure of justice to a savage leader, the ICC may have perpetuated, rather than ended, his crimes: Col. Gadhafi and his sons and generals do not dare end their campaign of violence if it means spending years in a Dutch cell."

Max Boot similarly argued that because of the ICC:

> "Qaddafi has every incentive to fight to the death and take a lot of people down with him."

Putting aside the problem of laying blame at the feet of the ICC rather than the UN [United Nations] Security Council, the argument, on some level, is compelling: why would individuals like Gaddafi negotiate an agreement which delivered them to the Hague? They wouldn't, the argument goes, and instead will have every incentive to continue committing atrocities.

Investigations Encourage Peace

The problem is, there's no real evidence of this. Indeed, some suggest that investigations and indictments may, in fact, provide incentives to negotiate. Take the case of the ICC's involvement in the situation in northern Uganda for example.

The ICC was heavily criticized for issuing arrest warrants for senior commanders of the Lord's Resistance Army (LRA), including the notoriously brutal Joseph Kony and Vincent Otti. Criticism centered around the court being an external imposition that risked undermining a fragile peace process

Accountability vs. Power-Sharing

Recent peace negotiations practice has given rise to the emergence of two paradigms. In line with normative developments in global human rights protection, internationally brokered peace processes often address the options for accountability for abuses committed in the past, and generally cannot include blanket amnesties. At the same time, many agreements end armed conflicts through offering power-sharing incentives for warring parties. In most cases, power-sharing arrangements are likely to clash with attempts to meaningfully deal with truth, accountability and reparation for past abuses. The tension between the two paradigms gives rise to a number of important challenges and constraints for policy makers and thus far there is little evidence from practice to guide them in managing the clash.

Chandra Lekha Sriram and Stef Vandeginste,
Power-Sharing and Transitional Justice:
A Clash of Paradigms?, *March 16, 2011.*
http://research.allacademic.com.

between the LRA and the government of Uganda. There was widespread support in civil society for the granting of amnesty to individuals in the LRA as an incentive to lay down their arms and reintegrate into society.

Then something unexpected happened. The LRA became more engaged in the peace process than it previously had been. A round of negotiations were set up in Juba, South Sudan, in 2006, just a year after the arrest warrants for Kony and others were issued. Some have called this the best opportunity in twenty years to finally establish peace in northern Uganda. Eventually, in 2008, the Juba peace talks failed. Some observers placed the blame on the ICC. But it remains unclear what the role of the arrest warrants was in the failure of the negotiations.

Regardless of what commentators may suggest, it is not obvious how ICC arrest warrants affect the behaviour of individuals like Gaddafi and Kony. However, it may be just as likely to give them the incentive to negotiate their immunity, exile or asylum as to "fight to the death".

None of this is to defend the ICC or its involvement in all contexts. But in the presumptuously labelled "peace *versus* justice" debate, there's a need to balance claims and counterclaims, to contrast competing versions of events, and to compare experiences across cases. There may be tensions between the pursuit of peace and the pursuit of justice but they are more murky than clear. Our understanding of these tensions is only hampered by simplistic narratives, however compelling or intuitive they may be.

Gaddafi's Supporters Must Be Included

Remarkably, no commentator to date has considered that the real clash of simultaneously pursuing justice and peace in Libya is not the result of some simple notion of conflict resolution as a bargaining process. Rather, it derives from the reality that a power-sharing agreement may be necessary and, at the moment, Gaddafi is the only one to negotiate with in Tripoli.

This brings up some uncomfortable realities. If not with Gaddafi himself, then the rebels and the international coalition behind them will have to negotiate with those who remain loyal to him. It is simply unfeasible for the prospects of peace in Libya that pro-Gaddafi factions are barred from the peace process. That may only create powerful spoilers of peace.

There may only be bad options to ensure that Gaddafi isn't at the other end of the peace negotiation table with the rebels: his death or a deal that includes impunity and exile/

asylum. Neither would be justice and one necessarily includes a round of direct negotiation with Gaddafi. Hope that Gaddafi would be deserted by all of those loyal to him has turned out to be just that: hope.

The international community is rightfully noncommittal to targeting Gaddafi. However, by doing so they are left with one option: negotiating Gaddafi's departure. This is evidently being considered as a "necessary evil".

The debate about the relationship between peace and justice remains dominated by simple narratives. We are told that either there is "no peace without justice" or that there is "no justice without peace"; either we are good and moral and thus support accountability everywhere, regardless of context or consequence, or we simply must sacrifice accountability because it plays second fiddle to peace. But it just isn't that simple and Libya is teaching us this lesson once again.

Periodical and Internet Sources Bibliography

The following articles have been selected to supplement the diverse views presented in this chapter.

Al Jazeera English	"Gaddafi Ordered Lockerbie Bombing," February 24, 2011. http://english.aljazeera.net.
Christopher Boucek	"Libyan State-Sponsored Terrorism: An Historical Perspective," Jamestown Foundation, May 5, 2005. www.jamestown.org.
Economist	"The Lockerbie Bomber's Release, Revisited: The Darkest Deal," February 10, 2011. www.economist.com.
Economist	"The Lockerbie Controversy: Friends Like These," August 27, 2009. www.economist.com.
Thomas Joscelyn	"The Libyan Terrorist: Muammar Qaddafi," *Weekly Standard*, February 24, 2011. www .weeklystandard.com.
David Leigh	"WikiLeaks Cables: Lockerbie Bomber Freed After Gaddafi's 'Thuggish' Threats," *Guardian*, December 7, 2010. www.guardian.co.uk.
Jenna Lyle	"Lockerbie Bomber Should Be Released, Says Church Minister," *Christian Today*, August 14, 2009. www.christiantoday.com.
RS Politics Daily (blog)	"Where Are Libya's WMD?" February 24, 2011. www.rollingstone.com.
Scott Stewart	"Libya's Terrorism Option," STRATFOR, March 23, 2011. www.stratfor.com.
Daniel Wagner and Daniel Jackman	"Libya's Path Back to Terrorism," *Huffington Post*, March 24, 2011. www.huffingtonpost.com.

OPPOSING
VIEWPOINTS®
SERIES

CHAPTER 4

What Should the US Role in Libya Be?

Chapter Preface

One of the most violent confrontations between Libya and the United States occurred in 1986. The administration of US president Ronald Reagan had already singled out Libya as a dangerous supporter of terrorism. The United States and Libya were also involved at the time in a territorial dispute over freedom of navigation in the Gulf of Sidra on the north coast of Libya. Libya had launched ineffective attacks on American shipping, and the United States had retaliated by sinking four Libyan attack ships.

The Reagan administration considered an assault on Libyan territory at several points, but after much discussion, held off. Finally, however, on April 14 a terrorist bombing of a discotheque in West Berlin killed two US servicemen and a Turkish woman. "Another 229 people were wounded, including 79 Americans" when a "two-kilogram bomb packed with plastic explosives and shrapnel exploded close to the dance floor," according to Nathalie Malinarich in a November 13, 2001, article on BBC News.

The Reagan administration said it had "irrefutable evidence of Libyan involvement" in the discotheque attack according to Ronald Bruce St. John in *Libya and the United States: Two Centuries of Strife*. (Fifteen years after the bombing, it was established that workers in the Libyan embassy in East Germany had been responsible for the attacks.)

Reagan, therefore, ordered air strikes on Tripoli and other sites in Libya. The bombings killed at least one hundred people, some in military bases, but others in the civilian suburb of Bin Ashur. "Colonel Muamar Gaddafi's residential compound took a direct hit that killed Hanna Gaddafi, the adopted baby daughter of the Libyan leader," according to an April 15, 1986, report by BBC News.

In a television address after the strikes, President Reagan characterized the military operation as an act of self-defense, stating, "When our citizens are attacked or abused anywhere in the world on the direct orders of a hostile regime, we will respond so long as I am in office." Many throughout the world, however, saw the assault as an unnecessary and deadly use of force. There were large-scale protests in London, Rome, Vienna, Bonn, West Berlin, and other cities. "We came to register massive public disgust at the bombing of Libya," said Bruce Kent, a clergyman and vice chairman of the Campaign for Nuclear Disarmament, as quoted in a March 20, 1986, article in the *Los Angeles Times* by Tyler Marshall. The raids were much more popular in the United States, however.

The goal of the attacks was to curb Libyan support for terrorism, and its success on that front is unclear. Ronald Bruce St. John argues that the strikes had little long-term effect on Libyan policy. William C. Martel in *Victory in War: Foundations of Modern Military Policy*, however, says that "the response of the Libyan government to the U.S. military raid was a brief spike in [support of terrorist] activity followed by a gradual decrease in, and apparent curtailment of, its support for terrorism."

The following viewpoints discuss the rising and falling tensions between the United States and Libya in more recent years.

| "The same Arab leaders who protect murderous despots ... have called on the West to take forceful action to oust Libya's leader."

The United States Should Intervene in Libya for Pragmatic and Humanitarian Reasons

James Traub

James Traub is a contributing writer for New York Times Magazine *and a columnist for ForeignPolicy.com. In the following viewpoint, he argues that Arab states have urged Western intervention in Libya. He says that this removes the major diplomatic obstacle to intervention. He argues that intervention would prevent the killing of civilians and would improve US standing in the region. He acknowledges that risks exist but argues that the overall benefits of intervention are worth it.*

As you read, consider the following questions:

1. What Arab organizations and rulers does Traub list as supporting Western intervention?

2. Why does Traub say a no-fly zone may not be the best strategy in Libya?

3. According to Traub, what do White House officials hope will happen in Libya?

In September 1999, in the aftermath of the brutal ethnic cleansing that Serbian forces had perpetrated on the civilian population of Kosovo, U.N. [United Nations] Secretary-General Kofi Annan addressed the General Assembly on the subject of humanitarian intervention. The struggle over the appropriate response to the atrocities, Annan said, had "revealed the core challenge to the Security Council and to the United Nations as a whole in the next century: to forge unity behind the principle that massive and systematic violations of human rights—wherever they may take place—should not be allowed to stand." Annan's speech was greeted rapturously in the West—but not in the developing world. Answering Annan in the General Assembly, President Abdelaziz Bouteflika of Algeria said bluntly that "interference in internal affairs may take place only with the consent of the state in question."

Human Rights vs. Sovereignty

The debate over intervention has gone around and around the same circle ever since. Western leaders and Western thinkers—including Annan, whose views were shaped far more by decades of international service than by his boyhood in Ghana—have argued for the moral imperative of intervention in various forms to prevent or stop atrocities. The ex-colonial countries of the developing world, meanwhile, have invoked the sanctity of state sovereignty. The universal adoption in 2005 of the principle of "the responsibility to protect" has blunted that divide somewhat by shifting the emphasis from the right of outsiders to intervene to the obligation of all states to prevent atrocities. But the debates over action in

Burma, Sudan, Zimbabwe, and elsewhere were dominated by the same threadbare claims of sovereignty. Effective action was impossible so long as the neighbors insisted on protecting the abusive tyrant.

Until now. In the debate over intervention in Libya, Russian diplomats have contented themselves with the usual boilerplate on sovereignty, but Arab states, remarkably, have not. The same Arab leaders who protect murderous despots like Sudanese President Omar Hassan al-Bashir have called on the West to take forceful action to oust Libya's leader, Muammar al-Qaddafi. In recent days, the Gulf Cooperation Council, as well as the leaders of the Arab League [officially the League of Arab States] and the Organization of the Islamic Conference, have called for the establishment of a no-fly zone over Libya. Soon after Qaddafi began his attacks on unarmed civilians, the Qatari foreign ministry, which maintains equable relations with virtually all parties to Middle East conflicts, issued a statement criticizing "the silence of the international community over the bloody events in Libya."

Of course, the fact that Libya's neighbors are calling for a no-fly zone doesn't, by itself, make it a good idea. After all, they're not proposing to do anything but vote on it; the actual work would most likely have to be done by the United States and NATO [North Atlantic Treaty Organization], which in practice means the United States, which has the air assets in the region. And Russia or China could still block Security Council authorization for further action. But in this case, the legitimacy of Arab bodies counts for much more than the council's authorization. Qaddafi will, of course, try to portray himself as the victim of a Western crusade. That would be a lot harder if both Libya's rebels and Arab leaders publicly call for the action, and stand by it (which is, of course, far from a certainty). Arab endorsement removes the single greatest political obstacle to action.

Violations of Human Rights Will Not Be Tolerated

Today the world's eyes are fixed on Libya. We have seen Colonel Qadhafi's security forces open fire on peaceful protestors again and again. They have used heavy weapons on unarmed civilians. Mercenaries and thugs have been turned loose to attack demonstrators. There are reports of soldiers executed for refusing to turn their guns on their fellow citizens, of indiscriminate killings, arbitrary arrests, and torture.

Colonel Qadhafi and those around him must be held accountable for these acts, which violate international legal obligations and common decency. Through their actions, they have lost the legitimacy to govern. And the people of Libya have made themselves clear: It is time for Qadhafi to go—now, without further violence or delay.

The international community is speaking with one voice and our message is unmistakable. These violations of universal rights are unacceptable and will not be tolerated.

Hillary Clinton, "Secretary Clinton's Remarks to the Human Rights Commission," RealClearPolitics.com, February 28, 2011. www.realclearpolitics.com.

Worth Doing

So should NATO oblige Libya's outraged neighbors? Quite apart from the stupendous tactical difficulties that U.S. Defense Secretary Robert Gates has raised, and which opponents of a no-fly zone have been happy to repeat—and which strike me as the kind of military hyperbole Colin Powell deployed to argue against intervention in Bosnia in 1993—a no-fly zone may be the wrong solution to the Libyan crisis. Although

Qaddafi's forces have made increasingly effective use of air-power, they would still enjoy a decisive military advantage over the rebels without it. U.S. pilots could find themselves in the sickening position of watching helplessly while Libyan ground forces pulverize their adversaries—as U.S. forces did over southern Iraq in the aftermath of the Gulf War.

There is no point in establishing a no-fly zone unless both the West and Arab leaders are prepared to take the next step. This would be the kind of air strikes that finally brought Slobodan Milosevic to heel in 1995 [in Bosnia]: strikes against troop concentrations, bunkers, air-defense systems, and the like. This would be an outright act of war, though one that did not put foreign boots on Libyan soil. The goal, of course, would not be to induce Qaddafi to come to the negotiating table—a Hitler-like *Götterdämmerung* [that is, an apocalyptic last stand] is much more likely—but to damage and demoralize his forces and thus tip the scales between the government and the rebels. That might not take long, but of course military planners have to think about worst-case scenarios. The rebels are very disorganized, and Qaddafi and his men are very desperate. And according to a recent *New York Times* report, Qaddafi has enough cash to keep paying his militias for a long time to come.

So is it worth doing? If a Western-led intervention had the full support of neighbors and if it had a reasonable chance of operational success, would it constitute a proper use of U.S. military resources? The question of who rules this desert state is not, after all, a matter of U.S. national security. And though Qaddafi has plainly committed terrible atrocities, they don't begin to compare with those perpetrated by Bashir or Zimbabwe's Robert Mugabe, or by the factions in the Democratic Republic of the Congo. So neither the strategic nor the humanitarian case for action is overwhelming. And to be effective, that action would require a serious commitment of military force. So again, why do it?

Because it would be the right thing, and because it would be good for the United States. It would be the right thing because U.S. and NATO force could stop a ruthless tyrant from killing his own people and bring his monstrous rule to an end. Western intervention in the Congo wouldn't have solved the problem, while military action in Darfur [Sudan] might well have provoked a massive backlash in the Islamic world. But Libya is a case where force could work and where it will be deployed only after noncoercive methods have proved unavailing, as the doctrine of the responsibility to protect requires. And it would redound to America's benefit because the United States would be placing its military power at the disposal of the Arab world in order to liberate Arab peoples.

A Choice Must Be Made

Of course, absolutely everything about such a plan could go wrong. The Arab League could change its mind once the rubble began to fly; an American plane could get shot down; missiles could go awry and kill civilians; a rebel victory could throw Libya into chaos, or sharia [Islamic law], or back into charismatic authoritarianism. Or surgical strikes, like a no-fly zone, could prove unavailing. What then? A full-scale intervention? (Answer: It's a moot point, because the neighbors would never approve it.) And since any of these things could happen, the dictates of prudence might argue that U.S. policy makers take a pass at the unprecedented invitation to act.

White House officials, of course, are hoping that the rebels will win on their own. So is everyone. But if the rebels keep floundering, as seems increasingly likely, President Barack Obama will have to choose either to act or to forego action. We have learned that his idealism is even more tempered by caution—by prudence—than we had initially thought. It's very hard to predict which way he'll go. I know which I would prefer.

> "Most of the people endorsing an attack
> know less about Libya than they do
> about playing the oboe."

The United States Should Not Intervene in Libya

Steve Chapman

Steve Chapman is a columnist and editorial writer for the Chicago Tribune. *In the following viewpoint, he argues that the United States should not interfere in Libya on behalf of the rebels. He argues that there is no way to make a limited commitment and that once the United States enters the conflict, it will be required to escalate. He also says that US intervention is likely to backfire, resulting in accusations of US imperialism and causing the people we are claiming to help to turn against us.*

As you read, consider the following questions:

1. What people does Chapman list as having endorsed intervention in Libya?

2. What does Chapman say was the result of the United States supplying weapons to rebels in Afghanistan?

3. What did Zogby International find about Arab opinion about the United States in a 2006 poll?

The civil war in Libya was barely under way before some American politicians were insisting the United States crash the party. We have been fighting in Afghanistan for nine years and Iraq for eight, but the typical Washington hawk views wars the way Hugh Hefner [founder of *Playboy* magazine] views buxom blondes: You can never have too many.

The current craze is for a no-fly zone to help remove [Libyan leader] Moammar Gadhafi. It's been endorsed by Republicans John McCain, Newt Gingrich, and Tim Pawlenty, as well as Independent Joe Lieberman and Democrat John Kerry. Defense Secretary Robert Gates has thrown cold water on the idea, but the president has not ruled out military intervention.

Reasons to Stay Away

Why would that be a mistake? Plenty of reasons:

Safe, limited measures may not be either. The war party assumes that keeping Libya's air force on the ground—or destroying it should it take flight—will be quick, simple, and painless. But Joint Chiefs of Staff Chairman Adm. Mike Mullen says a no-fly zone would be "an extraordinarily complex operation to set up." It would add costs to a federal budget that is already excessive.

Such operations can lead to American casualties, if our planes are shot down. Errant bombs can kill innocent bystanders, as happens often in Afghanistan. At that point, things suddenly get a lot messier.

Getting in is the easy part. Even perfectly executed operations may fail to turn the tide. Suppose we establish our no-fly zone and Gadhafi's forces proceed to rout the rebels. Do we slink away? Or do we up the ante? Once we start the fight, we may not be able to control when and how it ends. If things go wrong, we will be left with only bad choices.

President Barack Obama's Handling of Situation in Libya

	Approve %	Disapprove %	No opinion %
National adults	44	44	12
Republican	26	63	11
Independent	42	45	13
Democrat	61	28	11

Polls show the US public is split on Libya.

TAKEN FROM: Keith Koffler, "Today's Obama Poll/Libya," *White House Dossier* (blog), March 29, 2011. www.whitehousedossier.com.

We would be adding burdens to a military that is already overstretched. If the ongoing wars elsewhere have put unprecedented strain on our volunteer forces, do we really want to demand even more of them?

"The American military," reports the *New York Times* with dry understatement, "is privately skeptical of humanitarian gestures that put the lives of troops at risk for the cause of the moment, while being of only tenuous national interest." No kidding.

We don't know what we're doing. Most of the people endorsing an attack know less about Libya than they do about playing the oboe. Yet this group is willing to shoot first and ask questions later, forgetting that ignorance usually trumps good intentions.

The United States had plenty of direct experience dealing with Iraq before the 2003 invasion. The [George W.] Bush administration had more than a year to analyze and prepare for what awaited. But once we had toppled Saddam Hussein [the Iraqi dictator], we were hit with one nasty surprise after another.

In Libya, the unknown unknowns are legion. We could be helping to bring to power a government even worse than Gadhafi's or creating a new haven for Islamic terrorists. One option is shipping weapons to the rebels—kind of like what we did in Afghanistan following the 1979 Soviet invasion.

Those weapons, as fate would have it, helped bring the [radical Islamist and anti-American] Taliban to power.

Not About Us

We will inflame greater suspicion in the Arab world. Conservatives like to credit George W. Bush's Iraq crusade for spawning democratic movements in Arab nations. But most Arabs don't share that flattering opinion.

Following the Iraq war, Zogby International polls found that by 2006, only 12 percent of Arabs in six countries had a favorable attitude toward the U.S. Two out of three said democracy was not a genuine American goal in the Middle East.

We may harm the cause of those we want to help. One reason these new democratic movements have generated such broad enthusiasm is that they are homegrown—not fostered by Washington at the point of a gun.

"Right now, it's not about us, and I don't want it to be about us," says Christopher Preble, director of foreign policy studies at the libertarian Cato Institute. Once the U.S. attacks, many Arabs will see it as a fight between an Arab leader and the American imperialists bent on subjugating Muslims, not a heroic struggle by the Libyan people against a dictator.

The United States has had an eventful decade in the realm of military and foreign policy. During that time, we have discovered, at a dear cost, the limits to America's power to transform the world. But we can always learn that lesson again.

> "The U.S. and NATO have triggered a civil war in Libya, as their pretext for long-standing plans of military aggression."

US Intervention in Libya Is Based on Imperialist Motives

Mahdi Darius Nazemroaya

Mahdi Darius Nazemroaya is a Canadian sociologist and a research associate of the Centre for Research on Globalization (CRG), specializing on issues concerning the Middle East and Central Asia. In the following viewpoint, he argues that Western powers have long had imperial designs on Libya because of its strategic location and oil. He says that despite the recent normalization of relations with Libyan leader Muammar Gaddafi, the United States and European Union have been planning military intervention and regime change in Libya. He says the West should not interfere in the Libyan civil war, and that conflict in Libya benefits the Western powers, not the people of Libya.

As you read, consider the following questions:

1. Why does Nazemroaya say that the London Conference on Libya is a breach of international law?

Mahdi Darius Nazemroaya, "Libya and the Imperial Re-Division of Africa," *Global Research*, April 26, 2011. http://www.globalresearch.ca. Copyright © 2011 Mahdi Darius Nazemroaya. All rights reserved.

2. According to Nazemroaya, foreign workers in Libya came from what countries?

3. Why does Nazemroaya say that Gaddafi has exercised restraint in terms of violence against his own people?

Plans to attack Libya have been long-standing. The imperial war machine of the United States, Britain, France, Italy, and their NATO [North Atlantic Treaty Organization] allies is involved in a new military adventure that parallels the events that led to the wars against Yugoslavia [in the 1990s] and Iraq [2003–present]. The war machine has been mobilized under the cover of "humanitarian intervention."

In fact what the Pentagon and NATO have done is breach international law by intervening on the side of one of the combating parties in Libya in a civil war that they themselves have encouraged and fuelled. They have not protected civilians, but have launched a war against the Libyan regime in Tripoli and actively assisted the Benghazi-based Transitional [National] Council in fighting the Libyan military.

War in Libya Has Been Planned for Years

Before the rapprochement with Colonel [Muammar] Qaddafi, for years the U.S., Britain, France, and their allies worked to destabilize Libya. Confirmed by U.S. government sources, Washington attempted regime change in Tripoli several times. According to General Wesley Clark, former NATO commander, the Pentagon had active plans for launching a war against Libya.

The U.S. and its NATO allies are now embroiled in a new war which has the patented characteristics of the wars and invasions of Iraq and the former Yugoslavia.

A large naval armada off the shores of Libya has been bombing Libya for weeks with the declared objective of ousting the Libyan regime. At the same time, Libyan internal divisions are being fuelled.

Misinformation is systematically being spewed. Like Saddam Hussein [the dictator of Iraq] before him, the U.S. and the E.U. [European Union] have armed and helped Colonel Qaddafi. It is, therefore, important to hold the U.S. and the E.U. accountable for these weapon sales and the training of Libyan forces.

Also, like in Iraq, another Arab dictator was befriended by the U.S., only to be subsequently betrayed.

Prior to Iraq's rapprochement with the U.S., at the outset of the Iraq-Iran War, Saddam Hussein was a Soviet ally and considered an enemy by Washington.

The case of Colonel Qaddafi is in many regards similar. Ironically, Qaddafi had warned Arab leaders in 2008 at a meeting in Damascus under the auspices of the Arab League [officially the League of Arab States] about regime change. He pointed to the U.S. government's "bad habit" of betraying its Arab dictator friends:

> Why won't the [UN] Security Council investigate the hanging of Saddam Hussein? How could the leader of an Arab League state be hanged? I am not talking about Saddam Hussein's policies or our [meaning the other Arab leaders'] animosity towards him. We all had our disagreements with him. We all disagree with one another. Nothing unites us except this hall. Why is there not an investigation about Saddam Hussein's execution?

> An entire Arab government is killed and hung on the gallows—Why?! In the future it is going to be your turn too! [The rest of the Arab officials gathered start laughing.] Indeed!

> America fought alongside Saddam Hussein against [Ayatollah] Khomeini [in the Iraq-Iran War]. He was their friend. [US vice president Dick] Cheney was a friend of Saddam Hussein. [Donald] Rumsfeld, the [US] Defence secretary during the bombing of Iraq [in 2003], was a close friend of Saddam Hussein.

At the end they sold him out. They hung him. Even you [the Arab leaders] who are the friends of America—no I will say we—we, the friends of America, America may approve of our hanging one day.

At the end of the 1991 Gulf War, the U.S. deliberately encouraged open revolt against Saddam Hussein's regime, but stood back and watched as Saddam Hussein put down the Iraqi revolts by force.

In 2011, they have done the same thing against Qaddafi and his regime in Libya. Not only was the revolt in Libya instigated by Washington and its allies, the rebels have been supplied with weapons and military advisers.

When the U.S. and its allies triggered the anti-Saddam revolts in Baghdad in the wake of the Gulf War, "no-fly zones" over Iraq were established by the U.S., Britain, and France under the pretext of protecting "the Iraqi people from Saddam." For years Iraq was systematically attacked. The Iraqi Republic was bombed and its capabilities to defend itself were eroded.

Today, the U.S. and its allies have imposed a no-fly zone over Libya with the pretext of protecting "the Libyan people from Qaddafi." If they wanted to protect the Libyan people from Qaddafi, why did they arm Qaddafi in the first place? Why did they enter into business transactions in the wake of the 2006 and 2008 anti-government riots in Libya? There is much more to this narrative, which is part of a broader march to war.

The London Conference

The London Conference on Libya [held on March 29, 2011] reveals the true colours of the coalition formed against Libya. In a clear breach of international law, the U.S., Britain, France, Germany, and their allies are making decisions about the future of Libya ahead of any changes on the ground. Democracy is a bottom-up process and Libyan governance is an internal matter to be decided upon by the Libyans themselves. These decisions cannot be made by foreign powers that have been the staunch supporters of some of the worst dictatorships.

The nations gathered at the conference table in London have no right whatsoever to decide on whether Qaddafi must stay or go. This is a sovereignty right that only Libyans alone have. Their involvement in the civil war is a breach of international law, as is their siding with one of the camps in the civil war.

The London Conference on Libya can be likened to the Berlin Conference of 1884. Unlike 1884, this conference is aimed at dividing the spoils of war in Libya, instead of the direct carving up of an entire continent. Also, Washington, instead of staying away like in 1884, is the leading power in this new conference involving the affairs of the African continent.

The position of the U.S. and its Western European allies is very clear:

> U.S. Secretary of State Hillary Rodham Clinton and British Foreign Secretary William Hague led the crisis talks in London between 40 countries and institutions, all seeking an endgame aimed at halting Gadhafi's bloody onslaught against Libya's people.
>
> Although the NATO-led air strikes on Gadhafi's forces that began March 19 aren't aimed at toppling him, dozens of nations agreed in the talks that Libya's future does not include the dictator at the helm.
>
> "Gadhafi has lost the legitimacy to lead, so we believe he must go. We're working with the international community to try to achieve that outcome," Clinton told reporters. . . .

The London Conference on Libya, however, not only deals solely with Libya, but holds the blueprints to a new imperialist re-division of the entire Africa continent. Libya, which became a holdout when Qaddafi changed his mind, will be used to complete the "Union for the Mediterranean" and as a new bridgehead into Africa. This is the start of major steps that will be taken by the U.S. and the E.U. to purge the growing Chinese presence from Africa.

"Operation Odyssey Dawn"

The name "Operation Odyssey Dawn" is very revealing. It identifies the strategic intent and direction of the war against Libya.

The Odyssey is an ancient Greek epic by the poet Homer which recounts the voyage and trials of the hero Odysseus of Ithaca on his way home. The main theme here is the "return home."

The U.S. and the imperialist powers are on their own odyssey of "return" into Africa.

This project is also intimately related to the broader military agenda in southwest Asia and the drive into Eurasia, which ultimately targets Russia, China, and central Asia.

Washington's military agenda pertains to the African and the Eurasian landmass, namely a supercontinent known as the "World-Island." It is control of the World-Island that is the object of U.S. strategies.

The U.S. and NATO have triggered a civil war in Libya, as their pretext for long-standing plans of military aggression. A systematic media disinformation campaign, similar to the one used against Iraq from 1991 to 2003, has been launched.

In fact, the media has led the way for the war in Libya as it did in the former Yugoslavia, Afghanistan, and Iraq. The U.S. and its cohorts have also used the atmosphere of popular revolt in the Arab world as a cloud to insert and support their own agenda in the Libyan Arab Jamahiriya [that is, Libya].

There is an old Libyan proverb that says "if your pocket becomes empty, your faults will be many." In this context, Libyan internal tensions are not dominated by breadbasket issues. This sets Libya apart from Arab countries like Tunisia, Egypt, Yemen, Morocco, and Jordan. In Libya, the lack of freedom as well as rampant corruption has created opposition to the regime, which has been used by the U.S. and its allies as a pretext to justify foreign intervention.

Libya has come a long way since 1951 when it became an independent country. In 1975, the political scientist Henri Habib described these conditions:

> When Libya was granted its independence by the United Nations on December 24, 1951, it was described as one of the poorest and most backward nations of the world. The population at the time was not more than 1.5 million, was over 90% illiterate, and had no political experience or know-how. There were no universities and only a limited number of high schools which had been established seven years before independence.

According to Habib the state of poverty in Libya was the result of the yoke of Ottoman domination followed by an era of European imperialism in Libya. Habib explains: "Every effort was made to keep the Arab inhabitants [of Libya] in a servile position rendering them unable to make any progress for themselves or their nation." He also explains:

> The climax of this oppression came during the Italian administration (1911–1943) when the Libyans were not only oppressed by the [foreign] authorities, but were also subjected to the loss and deprivation of their most fertile land which went to colonists brought in from Italy. The British and French who replaced the Italians in 1943 attempted to entrench themselves in [Libya] by various divisive ways, ultimately to fail through a combination of political events and circumstances beyond the control of any one nation.

Despite political mismanagement and corruption, Libya's oil reserves (discovered in 1959) were used to improve the standard of living for its population. Libya has the highest standards of living in Africa.

In addition to its energy reserves, the Libyan state played an important role. Libyan energy reserves were nationalized after the 1969 coup against the Libyan monarchy [in which Qaddafi came to power]. It should be noted that these Libyan energy reserves are a source of wealth in Libya that if fully privatized would be a lucrative spoil of war.

To a certain extent, the isolation of Libya in the past as a pariah state has also played a role in insulating Libya. As most of the world has become globalized from an economic standpoint, Libyan integration into the global economy has in a sense been delayed.

Despite having vast sums of money stolen and squandered by Qaddafi's family and their officials, social services and benefits, such as government housing, are also available in Libya. It has to be cautioned too that none of this means that neoliberal restructuring and poverty are not afoot in Libya, because they very much are.

Until the conflict in 2011 ignited, there was a huge foreign work force in Libya. Thousands of foreign workers from every corner of the globe went to Libya for employment. This included nationals from Turkey, China, sub-Saharan Africa, Latin America, the European Union, Russia, Ukraine, and the Arab world.

Neoliberalism and the New Libya

From 2001 to 2003, a process of rapprochement began between Libya and the U.S. and its E.U. partners. What changed? Colonel Qaddafi did not stop being a dictator or change his behaviour. Rapprochement brought an end to Tripoli's defiance to its former colonial masters. Libya had bowed to U.S. and E.U. pressures and a modus vivendi came into effect.

Qaddafi's credentials as a democrat or a dictator were never an issue. Nor was the use of brute force. Subservience was the real issue.

The force used against the riots in 2006 and 2008 did not even faze the E.U. and Washington, which continued their "business as usual" with Tripoli. Even U.S. government sources

implied that economic interests should not be jeopardized by issues of international law or justice; for example, BP [British Petroleum] pressured the British government in 2007 to move forward with a prisoner exchange with Libya so that a Libyan oil contract could be protected.

Almost overnight, Libya became a new business bonanza for U.S. and E.U. corporations, especially in the energy sectors. These lucrative contracts also included military contracts of the order of $482 million (U.S.) in military hardware, training, and software from E.U. members (including chemical and biological agents).

Yet, two more things were demanded by Washington, namely the imposition of an imperial tribute as well as the opening up of the Libyan military and intelligence apparatus to U.S. influence. As a result Libya ended all support for the Palestinians and handed the U.S. government its dossiers on resistance groups opposed to Washington, London, Tel Aviv and their allies. This turned Libya into a so-called "partner" in the "Global War on Terrorism." . . .

Libya has also become active in global banking and finance. The U.S. Federal Reserve Bank of New York even made 73 loans to the Arab Banking Corporation (ABC), which is a bank mostly owned by the Central Bank of Libya, totalling an amount of $35 billion (U.S.). According to Senator Bernard Sanders of Vermont in a complaint to U.S. Treasury Secretary Timothy Geithner and U.S. Federal Reserve Chairman Benjamin Bernanke, the mostly Libyan-owned bank received over $26 billion (U.S.) in near-zero-interest-rate loans from the U.S. Federal Reserve that it has been lending back to the U.S. Treasury at a higher interest rate. The Arab Banking Corporation is currently exempted from sanctions on Libya and may serve in creating a fiscal link between Wall Street and Benghazi.

Saif al-Islam Qaddafi [one of Qaddafi's sons] was vital in this process of opening up Libya to trade with Washington and the European Union. In 2000 Saif al-Islam graduated from a university in Austria and became heavily tied to foreign associates who became his policy advisors and friends.

Prince Andrew of Britain reportedly became a close friend of Saif al-Islam: so close that Chris Bryant, a senior Labour Party politician, demanded in the British House of Commons that Prince Andrew be removed from his position as special trade envoy at the start of the conflict with Libya.

Western advisors to Tripoli played an important role in shaping Libyan policy. A "New Libya" started to emerge under Saif al-Islam, who pushed for the adoption of IMF [International Monetary Fund]-style neoliberal economic reforms.

Starting in 2005–2006, significant social and income disparities started to emerge in Libya. The Libyan Revolutionary Committees Movement was in large part disbanded by Saif al-

Islam. Had the Committees Movement remained, they would most probably have sought to prevent the present conflict from escalating.

Moreover, Saif al-Islam went to London and established ties in Britain with Noman Benotman, a former leader of the Libyan Islamic Fighting Group (LIFG). He became friends with Benotman.

Supported by Saif al-Islam, Benotman and Ali al-Sallabi, a Libyan citizen based in Qatar (who was on Tripoli's terrorist list), negotiated a truce between the Libyan Islamic Fighting Group and the Libyan government.

It is also worth noting that all the ministers and ambassadors who defected or left Libya were chosen by Saif al-Islam.

As in the case of the former Yugoslavia in the 1990s, the neoliberal reforms applied in Libya created social and income disparities which in turn contributed to political instability.

Rapprochement with Tripoli and Imperial Extortion

In late 2008, the U.S. government got Tripoli to pay what was tantamount to an "imperial tribute." Libya capitulated and agreed to an uneven reparation agreement with Washington. The agreement is called the "Claims Settlement Agreement between the United States of America and the Great Socialist People's Libyan Arab." Under the agreement Libya would concede $1.3 billion U.S. dollars to Washington, while Washington would give the Libyans $300 million U.S. dollars. . . .

Despite all this, Libya has remained a relatively wealthy country. In 2010, Tripoli even made an offer to buy a portion of British Petroleum (BP), one of the world's largest corporations. The National Oil Corporation of Libya also remains one of the largest oil companies in the world.

Even with the lucrative business deals that resulted from the rapprochement, the U.S. and the E.U. have always had an objective of furthering their gains and control. The E.U. powers and Washington merely waited for the right opportunity. Plans for taking over and controlling Libya and the Libyan energy sector were never abandoned. Nor could Washington and western Europe accept anything less than a full-fledged puppet government in Libya.

Even with the rapprochement with Tripoli, the U.S. and its E.U. partners continued to cultivate ties to so-called "opposition" figures and organizations with a view to implementing regime change at some future date. This is why the National Front for the Salvation of Libya has been mostly active in Washington. In the words of a timely Congressional Research Service (CRS) report (February 18, 2011):

> The National Conference for the Libyan Opposition . . . and Internet-based organizers called for a "day of rage" to take place on February 17. Similar events had been organized by anti-government groups in many other countries in the Middle East and North Africa over the previous month. On February 17, hundreds of protestors took to the streets in Benghazi and in other cities in its vicinity.

Colonel Qaddafi has ruled Libya under a harsh dictatorship that has systematically used violence and fear. Yet, the level of violence that has put Libya in a state of upheaval has been distorted. Many of the initial reports coming out of Libya in early 2011 were also unverified and in many cases misleading. These reports have to be studied very carefully. According to the same CRS report prepared for the U.S. Congress, initial reports all came from "local [Libyan] media accounts, amateur video footage and anecdotes, and reports from human rights organizations and opposition groups in exile."

Qaddafi's objectives are to preserve his regime and not to undo it. After Qaddafi became aware of the growing foreign threat directed towards his regime, the use of force was on the whole restrained. The regime in Tripoli did not want to give further excuses to the U.S., the E.U., and NATO for military intervention in Libya.

Qaddafi had exercised restraint for the sake of preserving his dictatorship. The Libyan regime knew very well that a bloody civil war would be used as a justification for intervention under a humanitarian pretext. That is why Qaddafi opted to try to negotiate where he could instead of using force. The use of violence is not to the favour of the Libyan regime or Libya, but rather works in the favour of the U.S. and the E.U. states.

| *"Should the world let Libyan civilians die at the hands of a tyrant?"*

US Intervention in Libya Has Nothing to Do with Imperialism

Ian Williams

Ian Williams is a senior analyst for Foreign Policy In Focus. In the following viewpoint, he argues that Arab nations and the Libyans themselves have called for international intervention to stop Libyan leader Muammar Gaddafi from killing civilians. Williams says that the West is bound to heed these calls. He also points out that intervention was sanctioned through the United Nations and is in accord with international law. He admits that the motives and actions of Western powers may not be perfect but argues that it is better to intervene imperfectly than to allow a massacre of Libyan civilians.

As you read, consider the following questions:

1. What does Williams say is the archetypal case of intervention in leftist lore?

2. According to Williams, why did Franklin Roosevelt do an end run around Congress in the years leading up to Pearl Harbor?

3. What is the "Israeli defense" at the United Nations, according to Williams?

It is a particularly pernicious form of cultural imperialism for comfortable Western leftists to disregard what the actual Tunisians, Libyans, Kosovars, or Bosnians themselves have asked for—intervention to stop "their" rulers' killing them. This setting aside of the wishes of people threatened with massacre in favor of Western armchair anti-imperialism is all the more remarkable coming from the left, which once swore by internationalism.

Should the World Let Libyans Die?

The calls to respect national sovereignty echo those of the despots of Africa and other regimes around the world who believe that it's nobody's business what a ruler does in his "own" country. Or even worse, such calls emulate the know-nothing isolationists on the right who do not care what happens to foreigners.

The ad-hoc arguments marshaled against the intervention in Libya have included:

- The unconstitutionality of the president ordering military action

- The expense of military action at a time of cuts

- The invalidity of a UN [United Nations] resolution passed with abstentions

- The Security Council exceeding its authority by violating Libyan sovereignty

- The self-interested motives of those intervening

- The "discovery" of ex-al Qaeda [the international terrorist group] supporters among the rebels

- The failure of the West to intervene in other places where civilians face potential massacres such as Bahrain, Gaza, Ivory Coast, and Yemen

Many of these arguments are deployed to flesh out an otherwise bald and unconvincing narrative that evades the crucial question: Should the world let Libyan civilians die at the hands of a tyrant?

Gaddafi's heavily armed forces were headed to Benghazi, in defiance of Security Council resolutions, to carry out acts against international humanitarian law. In fact, they had already started bombing and shelling the city indiscriminately and had a track record of massacres, mass arrests, and brutality in cities they had already occupied.

Intervention: Always Wrong?

Opposition to interventionism has sometimes been muted in other circumstances, for instance Vietnam's invasion of Cambodia and Laos, Tanzanian intervention in Uganda, or indeed India's military incursion that gave birth to Bangladesh. In none of these cases was the result utopian, but in each case it certainly improved the situation. Indeed Cuban intervention in Africa and Che's [that is, Che Guevara's] disastrous guerrilla escapades in Latin America are the subject of reverent leftist legend rather than calumny.

Perhaps the archetypal case, in leftist lore, is the Spanish Civil War. Few of those opposing intervention in Libya are likely fans of George Orwell who, after returning from Spain, commented that "there is hardly such a thing as a war in which it makes no difference who wins. Nearly always one side stands more or less for progress, the other side more or less for reaction." Orwell and many others went to Spain to fight [Spanish dictator Francisco] Franco and supported calls for intervention by the Western powers to help the Republic.

Orwell was also well aware of the imperfection of the side he was fighting for, since he not only witnessed the repression of dissidents on the Republican side but barely escaped with his life from KGB [Russian secret police] agents. Of course, the Spanish Republicans *should* have refused aid and weapons from the Soviet regime, which was already killing people in quantities that at the time exceeded what the Nazis were accomplishing. But nobody else was offering.

However, all the bluster notwithstanding, intervention, as now enshrined in the "Responsibility to Protect," is now an established part of international law. The intervention in Libya is legal. Whether it was the right thing to do, or whether the United States should be involved, is a separate issue, as indeed is the permanently debatable but entirely domestic issue of presidential versus congressional prerogatives on the matter of war powers.

A British or European might want to point out, however, that many of us are glad that Franklin Roosevelt did an end run round Congress in the years leading up to Pearl Harbor, even if his clear aim was to grab the British Empire before it fell into Axis hands. Indeed, the non-intervention rule is particularly ironic for the United States, which owes its independence to the timely intervention [in the American Revolution] of a reactionary French Royalist regime.

There would be more consistency, and indeed humanity, if protestors refined their arguments so they did not oppose intervention in general, but specified why they opposed intervention by particular countries, which in this case means the United States.

Should We Oppose US Involvement?

As a rule of thumb, one should always be wary of US intervention, and it is indeed always worth questioning both Washington's motives and its methods.

The United States Should Cut Off Relations with Repressive Regimes

When people cry for help you do what you can. And yes, what happened in Bahrain is shameful, even though the regime has yet to use airpower and artillery against its own city. So rather than opposing intervention in Libya, it would be much more constructive to call on the United States to cut off relations with Bahrain, or indeed Saudi Arabia, until the repression stops. But opposition is always easy, while calling for action involves taking responsibility for the results.

Ian Williams, "Strategic Dialogue: Libya War,"
Foreign Policy In Focus, *April 5, 2011. www.fpif.org.*

But the positions of many of those who have reflexively opposed the implementation of the UN resolution on Libya do not really involve questioning. Rather they consist of a series of dogmatic assertions, which tend to distill down to the assertion that the United States is *always* wrong. Even a stopped clock is right occasionally, and their assertion of perpetual American malice and greed is a form of metaphysical mirror image of the equally untenable premise that the United States is always virtuous and right.

In the case of Libya, as in Kosovo [where the United States intervened in the 1990s], the United States was dragged unwillingly into its role by the Europeans and others and by the events on the ground, namely Gaddafi's murderous threats and actual behavior. The United States had developed cynically good relations with Gaddafi. The West had no problems gaining access to Libyan oil. Regime change puts these relationships at risk.

Above all, the Security Council mandated this intervention, fulfilling its mandate to preserve peace and security, as interpreted by the General Assembly, which decided that that remit includes the failure of governments to protect their own people—or their persistence in attacking them.

UN Security Council Resolution 1973 was the classic smorgasbord that comes out of negotiations, with potential vetoes lurking in the background. To assuage the fears of those opposed to U.S. imperialism rightly concerned about what happened in Iraq [which the US invaded in 2003] (without a UN mandate), the resolution precluded troops on the ground. Sadly that left air operations as the only weapon. U.S. affection for massive firepower and force protection perhaps led to the unnecessarily massive bombardment of the first days. But on the other hand there has been no significant anti-aircraft action from Libya. Libyan geography has also lent itself to attacks on military columns strung out along the few roads with less risk of civilian casualties.

The mandate to protect civilians is at once limited—and flexible. If a regime shows no intention of stopping its repression and bloodshed, the mandate can't be fulfilled without getting rid of him.

Frankly, Libya and the world would not suffer from Gaddafi's departure.

Why Libya?

Frequently, opposition to intervention has depended, oddly, on the traditional "Israeli defense" at the UN. Israeli diplomats often argue that no one should criticize Israel when there are so many Arab states guilty of similar or worse atrocities. In this context, the West's silence and inaction—indeed, the complicity in the repression in Yemen, Bahrain, and Syria—preclude any action in Libya.

In the real world, of course, such an all-or-nothing approach translates into "nothing." In Libya, the deployment of aircraft, tanks, and artillery against civilians certainly goes a stage beyond the admittedly pernicious use of small arms in those other countries—not of course in Gaza [an area in conflict with Israel], but we know the circumstances there.

In fact, the UN-sanctioned intervention in Libya seems so far to have fulfilled the promise of the Responsibility to Protect. It averted the threatened massacre of the citizens of Benghazi by Gaddafi's supporters. It has so far crippled the regime's main strength, its heavy weaponry, so that the local Libyan opposition has been driving the former government forces out of city after city. So far, unless you take the word of the mendacious Gaddafi regime, there have also been minimum civilian casualties.

Humanitarian intervention under the auspices of the Responsibility to Protect (R2P) is indeed a dangerous tool, subject to expedient abuse. Which is why its proponents insisted it needed a UN mandate. The Libyan intervention has that. The Security Council needs to monitor its execution carefully, and it could do that much more effectively if Moscow, in particular, would stop flip-flopping.

Behind Russian discomfort over R2P is its all-too-apparent relevance to Chechnya. But Moscow could have vetoed the resolution. Its abstention implicitly went along with the wording of the resolution, and its experience of the Gulf War resolutions taught it what to watch out for in terms of mission creep. If it stopped grandstanding and got more actively involved, it would be a better watchdog.

Gaddafi's is clearly a failed regime. Its collapse in almost every population center when challenged demonstrates a lack of popular and institutional support. The provisional government in Benghazi has claimed democratic principles and has so far lived up to them. There are some strange stirrings of Islamophobia among anti-interventionists who claim either that intervention is anti-Islamic or that the new government will be fundamentalist Islamic.

In any case, the rebels seem to have popular support. Those who respect popular sovereignty, as opposed to state sovereignty, should really let the Libyans decide whether it is better to die in a flood of tanks and rockets, or overcome them by calling for international aid.

| *"Demanding that the US take owner-ship of every crisis will assure only one outcome: failure."*

The United States Should Not Lead in Libya

Graham Allison

Graham Allison is the director of Harvard's Belfer Center for Science and International Affairs and a former assistant secretary of defense. In the following viewpoint, he argues that Europe should take the lead in dealing with the Libyan crisis and that the United States should play a supportive role. He says that Europe is physically closer to Libya than the United States is, and historically Europe has more experience and expertise in dealing with North African affairs. He concludes that the United States cannot solve every crisis and that giving more responsibility to Europe will create a safer and more secure world.

As you read, consider the following questions:

1. Where is Lampedusa located, and why is this significant, according to Allison?

2. What is the Rapid Deployment Force, and how does Allison argue that it should be used?

3. Does Allison believe that the United States has the capacity to impose a no-fly zone over Libya, and what evidence does he provide to back up his opinion?

President [Barack] Obama should announce immediately full U.S. support for a British-French-led no-fly zone [preventing any military flights] over Libya. He should express confidence in the British and French to organize and conduct this military operation with the backing of their colleagues in the 27-nation European Union and NATO [North Atlantic Treaty Organization]. The US should stand ready to respond to requests for help if we have unique capabilities, including intelligence assets, essential for this mission.

Defer to Europe

Moreover, President Obama should assure our British and French allies that if they decide to act without United Nations authorization, the United States will stand behind them—even as he reaffirms his hope that the Security Council will quickly authorize a no-fly zone.

Five major considerations make US deference to a European-led undertaking America's best option.

First, look at the map. Geographically, North Africa [where Libya is located] is to Europe as the islands of the Caribbean are to the U.S. The Italian isle of Lampedusa, where refugees are arriving by boat daily, is closer to Tunisia [a North African state] than the 90 miles from Cuba to Florida. Europeans cannot escape the direct and immediate consequences of whatever transpires across this small pond. Given this reality, their leaders are passionately calling for action and should be encouraged to act.

Second, history as well as geography has taught Europeans many complexities of culture, ethnicity, tribes, and personalities in the dramas unfolding in North Africa. How many members of Congress, or American TV anchors and editorialists, know which countries the following cities are in: Constantine, Meknes, Muscat, Sfax, Barqa, and Homs? How many Americans can name the major tribes that serve as the primary bond of allegiance in these countries?

Third, Europe has the military resources to do the job. When Europeans were unable to mount their own military campaign to stop slaughter in the Balkans during the late 1990s, the US was forced to act. To fill this capabilities gap, Britain and France announced creation of a joint Rapid Deployment Force of 60,000 troops. Its stated rationale was to give Europe a rapid reaction capacity to address contingencies directly impacting the continent. What more appropriate opportunity than the current conflict in Libya for Europe to use this instrument?

Fourth, in the aftermath of the fall of autocrats in Tunisia, Egypt, and Libya, new governments in these countries will require substantial, sustained financial and technical assistance to build more stable, prosperous, and democratic societies. Europe has the motivation and the resources to take the lead in what will require a multibillion-dollar decade or longer effort. Through the World Bank, International Monetary Fund, and well-established bilateral channels, the US should be fully supportive. But as it did for its Eastern European neighbors after the fall of the Berlin Wall, Europe should lead and provide the lion's share of the resources to meet the challenges that will follow the fall of the Wall of Arab Autocrats.

A More Intelligent Future

Finally, unlike Europe, the US is inescapably a global superpower with responsibilities that span every continent. The US cannot, however, serve in every place at every time as the world's policeman, fireman, and emergency management ser-

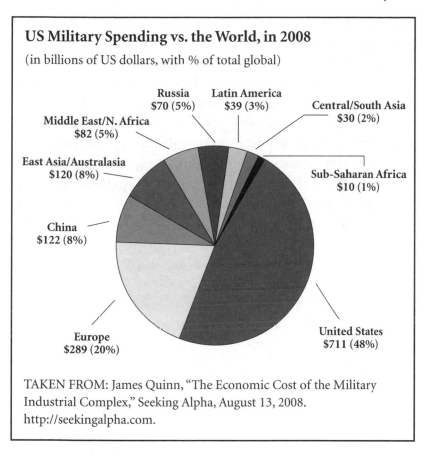

US Military Spending vs. the World, in 2008

(in billions of US dollars, with % of total global)

Russia $70 (5%)
Latin America $39 (3%)
Central/South Asia $30 (2%)
Middle East/N. Africa $82 (5%)
East Asia/Australasia $120 (8%)
Sub-Saharan Africa $10 (1%)
China $122 (8%)
Europe $289 (20%)
United States $711 (48%)

TAKEN FROM: James Quinn, "The Economic Cost of the Military Industrial Complex," Seeking Alpha, August 13, 2008. http://seekingalpha.com.

vice. Demanding that the US take ownership of every crisis will assure only one outcome: failure.

Success in meeting both current and future challenges will require smarter strategy and deeper collaboration with allies. This begins with internalizing a big strategic idea: the division of labor. By empowering states whose interests and values are sufficiently aligned with our own and encouraging them to take the lead in managing immediate and direct threats to their interests, the US will be better prepared to act in cases that require singular American leadership.

Could the U.S. unilaterally and decisively impose a no-fly zone over Libya? Of course. With an annual defense budget of

$700 billion, the U.S. has unrivaled global military reach that provides a capacity to go anywhere and destroy anything.

Why then has Secretary of Defense [Robert] Gates voiced such vehement opposition to the U.S. imposing a no-fly zone? His message is less about resources than about strategy. From that perspective, the current crisis in Libya represents an opportunity to begin the transition from the presumption that the US should always take the lead in meeting every global challenge. Recognizing Europe's interests, responsibilities, and capabilities to act in Libya points the way for a more intelligent and sustainable future.

| "But I am convinced when they are forced to deal with Libya themselves, the Europeans will get the job done."

The European Union, Not NATO, Should Lead in Libya

Sarwar Kashmeri

Sarwar Kashmeri is the author of NATO 2.0: Reboot or Delete? *and a fellow of the Foreign Policy Association. In the following viewpoint, he argues that the North Atlantic Treaty Organization (NATO) is often ineffective and is too closely associated with the United States. On the other hand, he says, the European Union (EU) has proved repeatedly over the past years that it can handle complicated military endeavors. Kashmeri concludes that the United States should hand responsibility for the Libyan conflict over to the EU, not NATO. He adds that this precedent will help encourage Europe to take responsibility for other military engagements in the future.*

As you read, consider the following questions:

1. What is CSDP, and why was it started, according to Kashmeri?

2. What was EUFOR Chad/CAR?

3. According to Kashmeri, what problem does Turkey present to European Union control of the Libyan conflict?

The Libyan war has illuminated NATO's [North Atlantic Treaty Organization's] dysfunctional structure and presents the United States with a unique opportunity to permanently change the way Europe handles its end of the transatlantic security bargain. America should grab the opportunity by turning over the conduct of the Libyan war to the European Union's [EU's] Common Security and Defense Policy (CSDP)—the EU's crisis management arm—and exit this conflict. That will be good for America, for Europe, and ultimately in the best interest of the wider transatlantic alliance. As President Obama told the nation on March 28, 2011, "... the burden of action should not be America's alone."

Work Through CSDP

CSDP was jump-started in 1999 by Britain and France—the same countries that led the charge for Libyan intervention—in response to the EU's inability to handle the Balkan conflicts in Europe's backyard. Using CSDP's military planning, command and control resources the EU has already deployed 27 successful CSDP military-civilian missions from Asia to Africa in the last decade.

Two of the larger CSDP missions illustrate the EU's military capabilities.

EU NAVFOR, launched in 2008, is the EU's first naval mission. It protects shipping off the coast of Somalia and is twice the size of NATO's anti-piracy force. More relevant to the Libyan situation was EUFOR Chad/CAR which deployed, and sustained, a powerful fighting force of 3,800 in the middle of Africa, thousands of miles from Brussels [Belgium], for 19 months. The force operated under a United Nations mandate to protect over 400,000 refugees, and operated over an area twice the size of France. The Naval mission continues. The mission to Africa accomplished its objectives and handed control to a United Nations force in March 2009. Interestingly, France played a leading role in the success of the EU's military intervention in Africa, as it is doing in Libya.

NATO played no role in organizing the sizable Chad mission. In fact, the government of Chad had made it clear NATO was not welcome there because it is widely seen as an extension of the United States. Sentiments that echo the reason some of the Europeans do not wish to see NATO take the leadership of the Libyan mission for fear of alienating the Arabs.

The Europeans Can Handle Libya

Neither NATO nor CSDP have their own military assets. Both use ships, airplanes and soldiers drawn mostly from EU countries. The British and French fighter jets now flying in Libya could just as easily belong to CSDP as to NATO. So, the EU already has the firepower to continue maintaining the no-fly zone over Libya and to confront Libya's military machine. It does not need American military assets in this one-sided battle against a minor military power. Of no less significance for cash-strapped American taxpayers is the fact that the EU is the world's largest provider of developmental aid which the Libyans will surely need after the shooting stops.

It is true that Turkey [which is a member of NATO] is not a member of the EU and is critically important to resolving the Libyan civil war. But I would leave it to the Europeans to sort out this symbiotic partnership. They will get it done. After all, in their African deployment, Russian military assets were integrated into an EU command structure that was led by a French general in the field and reported through an Irish general in France to the European Council which exercised ultimate political control. Talk about a politically charged command chain!

During the research for my forthcoming book on NATO, I spoke to over 50 military and political leaders on both sides of the Atlantic. I made it a point to ask some of the senior-most military leaders of the EU if, with CSDP, Europe now had the means to defend itself and to act militarily in Europe's periphery. Their answer was always in the affirmative, with one proviso—providing "we have the will."

The politics would be unnerving for a while. But I am convinced when they are forced to deal with Libya themselves, the Europeans will get the job done, as they have done 27 times in the last decade.

The EU has the military means to handle its own security. All it needs is the will, and Libya provides the opportunity for America to give Europe that will.

> "Even against an enemy as weak as Libya, NATO needs the backbone of U.S. might to fight effectively."

Without US Leadership, the Libyan Mission Is Failing

Robert Burns

Robert Burns writes about national security for the Associated Press. In the following viewpoint, he argues that the North Atlantic Treaty Organization (NATO) has struggled in Libya following the US handoff of the mission. Burns says that NATO is not used to leading missions without full US involvement. He also points out that US defense spending is much higher than anyone else's in the world and that, as a result, the United States has capabilities others lack. Even if the Libyan mission is ultimately successful, he concludes, it would have been brought to a close much quicker with US leadership.

Editor's note: Libyan dictator Muammar Gaddafi was captured and killed by rebel forces near his hometown of Sirte on October 20, 2011.

As you read, consider the following questions:

1. When and why was NATO created, according to Burns?

2. According to the viewpoint, what percentage of NATO's defense spending did the United States account for ten years ago, and how much does it account for today?

3. What non-European nations does Burns say (besides the United States) are involved in the Libyan mission?

President Barack Obama's insistence that NATO [North Atlantic Treaty Organization], not the U.S., take the lead in attacking Moammar Gadhafi's military is exposing a hard truth about an alliance that never before fought an air campaign with the U.S. in a back seat. Even against an enemy as weak as Libya, NATO needs the backbone of U.S. might to fight effectively.

It's not a matter of NATO's 27 non-U.S. member countries having too few combat aircraft, pilots or bombs. The problem instead is that while some, such as France and Britain, are willing to participate fully, others have limited their roles to noncombat action, and still others have decided not to participate militarily at all.

All have grown accustomed to a far different alignment— one in which the U.S. leads the way and bears the bulk of the combat burden. That's not a surprise, given that NATO was created in 1949 as a U.S.-led bulwark against the threat of an invasion of western Europe by the former Soviet Union.

Libya was supposed to be different.

In his March 28 [2011] speech explaining the mission to the American public, Obama described Libya as an instructive example of a problem that does not directly threaten American security. That means that while the U.S. should help protect civilians there, it should not have to bear the burden on its own, Obama said.

"Real leadership creates the conditions and coalitions for others to step up as well; to work with allies and partners so that they bear their share of the burden and pay their share of the costs," Obama said. He said he was fully confident that

NATO, as "our most effective alliance," would be able to "keep the pressure on" those Gadhafi ground forces that had not already been destroyed or damaged in an initial U.S.-led air assault.

At the time of his speech, NATO had just announced the decision to assume full responsibility for commanding the Libya operation, with the U.S. providing support such as flying most of the aircraft that provide surveillance and reconnaissance of the battlefield, as well as flying planes to refuel NATO jets.

"Because of this transition to a broader, NATO-based coalition, the risk and cost of this operation—to our military and to American taxpayers—will be reduced significantly," Obama said.

But how effective has it turned out to be, with a reduced American role?

Gadhafi has not been stopped from pressing the fight against Misrata—the only major city in the western part of Libya that is partially held by rebels—nor have NATO jets succeeded in rolling back those Gadhafi forces that threatened the eastern city of Ajdabiya.

Rebel hopes for a military victory have faded amid pleas for a more aggressive NATO and U.S. air campaign, and even some NATO allies are complaining about a half-hearted effort. Some of the alliance members are sniping at one another, and some are laying blame for the military stalemate at the U.S. doorstep.

Hans Binnendijk, vice president for research at the National Defense University and a leading U.S. authority on NATO, said Wednesday it is now clear that Obama's decision to draw back the U.S. military into a secondary role in Libya carried an implied challenge to NATO: "Let's see what you can do."

"And it may well be a sobering lesson for the Europeans to recognize that it is very hard for them to do these operations without the United States," he said in an interview.

Not least among the reasons for his conclusion: The gap between defense spending by the U.S. and its allies is enormous. NATO Secretary General Anders Fogh Rasmussen is fond of saying that whereas 10 years ago the U.S. accounted for just under half of NATO members' defense spending, it now is close to 75 percent. And the gap is likely to continue to grow, the NATO chief said, even with expected U.S. spending reductions.

That explains why, in Libya, the U.S. turns out to have performed more attack missions than it led many to believe it would after the April 4 handoff to NATO control. Pentagon officials on Wednesday disclosed that since the handoff, U.S. electronic warfare planes—with capabilities unmatched by any NATO ally—have dropped bombs on three occasions against Libya surface-to-air missile targets. Those missions have helped keep the skies clear for NATO to fly air patrols designed to keep Gadhafi's air force grounded.

Asked whether the U.S. might be persuaded to resume a larger role, State Department spokesman Mark Toner said questions relating to NATO's efforts would be addressed during a meeting of the alliance's foreign ministers Thursday and Friday in Berlin. But Toner suggested that the U.S. is not reconsidering.

"We believe NATO is fully capable of carrying out this mission," Toner said.

Obama's decision to withdraw from offensive air operations earlier this month was a calculated gamble that the Europeans, with help from Canada and non-NATO members Qatar and the United Arab Emirates, could accomplish the mission of protecting Libyan civilians without U.S. combat power. They may yet succeed, but what has become clear in recent days is that it probably will take longer than if the U.S. had stayed at the forefront.

Periodical and Internet Sources Bibliography

The following articles have been selected to supplement the diverse views presented in this chapter.

Amnesty International   "Q&A: Human Rights and War in Libya," March 21, 2011. www.amnesty.org.

BBC News   "Libya Sees 'Limited Improvements' in Human Rights," December 12, 2009. http://news.bbc .co.uk.

Juan Cole   "Qaddafi Using Cluster Bombs on Civilian Areas," *Informed Comment* (blog), April 15, 2011. www.juancole.com.

Maria Dimitrova   "Long-Awaited Acknowledgement of Bulgarian Nurses in Libya Innocence," Radio Bulgaria, February 24, 2011. http://bnr.bg.

Molly Hennessy-Fiske   "Libya: Human Rights Lawyer on Kadafi Warrant Impact on Arab Spring," *Babylon & Beyond* (blog), *LA Times*, May 17, 2011. http://latimesblogs.latimes.com/babylonbeyond.

Human Rights Watch   "Landmines in Libya: Technical Briefing Note," May 10, 2011. www.hrw.org.

Human Rights Watch   "Truth and Justice Can't Wait," December 12, 2009. www.hrw.org.

Meredith Jessup   "UN Council to Praise Libya's Human Rights Record," *The Blaze*, February 28, 2011. www .theblaze.com.

Tom Kuntz   "Libya's Late, Great Rights Record," *New York Times*, March 5, 2011. www.nytimes.com.

Siddhartha Mahanta   "Libya Lobbyists Come Clean," *Political MoJo* (blog), *Mother Jones*, May 6, 2011. http:// motherjones.com/mojo.

For Further Discussion

Chapter 1

1. The viewpoint by the United Nations Human Rights Council suggests that Libya has made strides in improving its human rights record. The US Department of State, however, argues that Libya's human rights record needs much improvement. Which viewpoint makes the stronger argument? Cite examples from the viewpoints to support your answer.

2. Consider the viewpoint by Human Rights Watch. Are human rights an important consideration in wartime? Is war itself a violation of human rights? Is there a way to conduct a war without violating human rights? Explain your answers.

Chapter 2

1. Iran is currently working on developing nuclear weapons. Based on the viewpoints in this chapter, do you think Libya's experience in giving up weapons of mass destruction (WMDs) would encourage Iranian leaders to build a bomb or discourage them from doing so? Explain your answer.

2. Based on Scott Stewart's argument, would *any* war be a boost for terrorism? Is there something special about the Libyan war that makes it particularly beneficial for terrorists?

Chapter 3

1. The viewpoint by Amir Taheri argues that the United States should help Libyan rebels by providing them with weaponry. Daniel R. DePetris believes that arming the

rebels would be a mistake. With which viewpoint do you agree? Cite examples from that viewpoint to support your answer.

2. Based on the viewpoints by US Africa Online and Michael J.K. Bokor, should the rebels and/or the United States agree to peace talks with Gaddafi? Explain your reasoning.

Chapter 4

1. Ian Williams argues that the people who claim that US actions in Libya are imperialistic are comfortable Western leftists. Is Mahdi Darius Nazemroaya a comfortable Western leftist? Is Williams? Does the fact that someone is a comfortable Western leftist mean that he or she should not express an opinion on these issues? Explain your answer.

2. Look at the viewpoints by Graham Allison, Sarwar Kashmeri, and Robert Burns. Is the United States' role as a world leader compromised if it does not take the lead in military operations in Libya? Is US pride at stake, or should these decisions be made on a pragmatic basis? Explain your answer.

Organizations to Contact

The editors have compiled the following list of organizations concerned with the issues debated in this book. The descriptions are derived from materials provided by the organizations. All have publications or information available for interested readers. The list was compiled on the date of publication of the present volume; names, addresses, phone and fax numbers, and e-mail and Internet addresses may change. Be aware that many organizations take several weeks or longer to respond to inquiries, so allow as much time as possible.

AhlulBayt Islamic Mission (AIM)
PO Box 2168 Watford, Hertfordshire   WD18 1BT
  UK
020 33 95 55 95
website: www.aimislam.com

AhlulBayt Islamic Mission (AIM) is a nonprofit Shia Islamic organization with worldwide membership that works to adopt Islam as a source of enlightenment and promote peace, justice, and social improvement for Muslims and non-Muslims alike. It promotes Islamic education and sociopolitical awareness and also provides services for young Muslims. Its website includes news and analysis, including articles on Libya such as "Ali Khalifa Far Worse than Gaddafi" and "Unacceptable Choices in Libya."

Brookings Institution
1775 Massachusetts Avenue NW
Washington, DC   20036-2188
(202) 797-6000
e-mail: communications@brookings.edu
website: www.brookings.edu

Brookings Institution, founded in 1927, is a liberal think tank that conducts research and education in foreign policy, economics, government, and the social sciences. It publishes numerous books and the quarterly *Brookings Review*. Its website includes numerous papers and articles, including "Libya and the Responsibility to Protect" and "The Future of Libya: A View from the Opposition."

Cato Institute

1000 Massachusetts Avenue NW
Washington, DC   20001-5403
(202) 842-0200 • fax: (202) 842-3490
website: www.cato.org

Cato Institute is a libertarian public policy research foundation dedicated to increasing the understanding of public policies based on the principles of limited government, free markets, individual liberty, and peace. It publishes the triannual *Cato Journal*, the periodic *Cato Policy Analysis*, and a bimonthly newsletter, *Cato Policy Review*. The website also includes articles such as "More Sensible Voices on Libya" and "The War in Libya and Limited Government."

Council on Foreign Relations

The Harold Pratt House, 58 East 68th Street
New York, NY   10065
(212) 434-9400 • fax: (212) 434-9800
website: www.cfr.org

The Council on Foreign Relations researches the international aspects of American economic and political policies. Its journal, *Foreign Affairs*, published five times a year, provides analysis on global conflicts. Articles on its website include "U.S. Military Intervention for Libya?" and "The Battle for Libya."

Human Rights Watch (HRW)

350 Fifth Avenue, 34th Floor, New York, NY   10118-3299
(212) 290-4700 • fax: (212) 736-1300
e-mail: hrwnyc@hrw.org
website: www.hrw.org

Human Rights Watch (HRW) is an international organization dedicated to ensuring that the human rights of individuals worldwide are observed and protected. To achieve this protection, HRW investigates allegations of human rights abuses and then works to hold violators, be it governments or individuals, accountable for their actions. The organization's website is divided by continent, offering specific information on individual countries and issues. It includes numerous reports on human rights in Libya.

International Criminal Court (ICC)

PO Box 19519, The Hague   2500 CM
  The Netherlands
+ 31 (0)70 515 8515 • fax: +31 (0)70 515 8555
website: www.icc-cpi.int/

The International Criminal Court (ICC) is an independent international organization established as the first permanent, treaty-based, international criminal court to help end impunity for the perpetrators of the most serious crimes of concern to the international community. The website includes information and articles about cases heard in the past as well as those currently before the court.

International Institute for Strategic Studies (IISS)

1850 K Street NW, Suite 300, Washington, DC   20006
(202) 659-1490 • fax: (202) 296-1134
website: www.iiss.org

The International Institute for Strategic Studies (IISS) is a leading world authority on political-military conflict. It has an international membership and focuses on researching and distributing information about international strategic issues. Its publications include the *Military Balance*, an annual assessment of 170 countries' defense capabilities, and *Survival: Global Politics and Strategy*, a bimonthly journal. Its website includes reports and analyses such as a video of Franco Frattini, Italy's minister of foreign affairs, speaking about international security and the Libya crisis.

North Atlantic Treaty Organization (NATO)

Boulevard Leopold III, Brussels   1110
  Belgium
website: www.nato.int

The North Atlantic Treaty Organization (NATO) is an inter-governmental military alliance including the United States and many European nations. It safeguards the safety and freedom of member countries through military and political means. Its website features news releases, speeches, transcripts, and other information, including a substantial section on NATO and Libya.

US Department of State, Bureau of Near Eastern Affairs

2201 C Street NW, Washington, DC   20520
(202) 647-4000
website: www.state.gov/p/nea/

The Bureau of Near Eastern Affairs, part of the US Depart-ment of State, deals with US foreign policy and US relations with the countries in the Middle East and North Africa. Its website offers country information as well as news briefings, press statements, and transcripts of congressional testimony, such as the statement of Harold Hongju Koh, the legal adviser of the Department of State, "Libya and War Powers."

Washington Institute for Near East Policy

1828 L Street NW, Suite 1050, Washington, DC   20036
(202) 452-0650 • fax: (202) 223-5364
e-mail: info@washingtoninstitute.org
website: www.washingtoninstitute.org

The Washington Institute for Near East Policy is an indepen-dent, nonprofit research organization that provides informa-tion and analysis on the Middle East and US policy in the re-gion. It publishes numerous books, periodic monographs, and reports on regional politics, security, and economics. Its web-site includes articles such as "Reforming the Rogue: Lessons from the U.S.-Libya Rapprochement."

Bibliography of Books

Peter L. Bergen — *The Longest War: The Enduring Conflict Between America and Al-Qaeda*. New York: Free Press, 2011.

Wyn Q. Bowen — *Libya and Nuclear Proliferation: Stepping Back from the Brink*. New York: Routledge, 2006.

Daniel Byman — *Deadly Connections: States That Sponsor Terrorism*. New York: Cambridge University Press, 2005.

Jack Caravelli — *Beyond Sand and Oil: The Nuclear Middle East*. Santa Barbara, CA: Praeger Security International, 2011.

Valya Chervenyashka and Nikolay Yordanov — *Notes from Hell: A Bulgarian Nurse in Libya*. Johannesburg, South Africa: 30° South Publishers, 2010.

Joseph Cirincione, Jon B. Wolfsthal, and Miriam Rajkumar — *Deadly Arsenals: Nuclear, Biological, and Chemical Threats*. Rev. ed. Washington, DC: Carnegie Endowment for International Peace, 2005.

John Crawford — *The Lockerbie Incident: A Detective's Tale*. Victoria, British Columbia: Trafford, 2002.

Mohamed ElBaradei — *The Age of Deception: Nuclear Diplomacy in Treacherous Times*. New York: Metropolitan Books, 2011.

Muammar Gaddafi and Edmond Jouve	*My Vision*. London: John Blake, 2005.
Richard A. Marquise	*Scotbom: Evidence and the Lockerbie Investigation*. New York: Algora Publishing, 2006.
Luis Martínez	*The Libyan Paradox*. Trans. John King. New York: Columbia University Press, 2007.
Khalil I. Matar and Robert W. Thabit	*Lockerbie and Libya: A Study in International Relations*. Jefferson, NC: McFarland and Co., 2004.
Bruce Riedel	*The Search for Al Qaeda: Its Leadership, Ideology, and Future*. Washington, DC: Brookings Institution Press, 2008.
Joseph T. Stanik	*El Dorado Canyon: Reagan's Undeclared War with Qaddafi*. Annapolis, MD: Naval Institute Press, 2003.
Ronald Bruce St. John	*Libya: Continuity and Change*. New York: Routledge, 2011.
Ronald Bruce St. John	*Libya: From Colony to Independence*. Oxford, UK: Oneworld Publications, 2008.
Ronald Bruce St. John	*Libya and the United States: Two Centuries of Strife*. Philadelphia: University of Pennsylvania Press, 2002.

Kimberly L. Sullivan — *Muammar Al-Qaddafi's Libya.* Minneapolis, MN: Twenty-First Century Books, 2009.

Dirk Vandewalle — *A History of Modern Libya.* New York: Cambridge University Press, 2006.

Dirk Vandewalle, ed. — *Libya Since 1969: Qadhafi's Revolution Revisited.* New York: Palgrave Macmillan, 2008.

John Wright — *The Emergence of Libya: Selected Historical Essays.* London: Silphium Press, 2008.

John Wright — *A History of Libya.* New York: Columbia University Press, 2010.

Index